Cordon Bleu

Fish 2

Macdonald and Jane's
London

Published by
Macdonald and Jane's Publishers Ltd
Paulton House
8 Shepherdess Walk
London N1

This impression 1977

Designed by Melvin Kyte
Printed by Waterlow (Dunstable) Ltd

These recipes have been adapted from the Cordon Bleu Cookery Course
published by Purnell in association with the London Cordon Bleu Cookery
School
Principal : Rosemary Hume ; Co-Principal : Muriel Downes

Contents

Introduction

This is our second book of fish dishes and the recipes this time are slightly more advanced than the first. This need not deter beginners, though, for the instructions are as full as usual and we have repeated the basic methods of cleaning and filleting fish.

Fish is a wonderful food and tends to be unworthily neglected in Britain. Whether you choose a white fish, a richer, oily fleshed fish or one of the delicious, delicate shellfish from around our shores, you can be sure of a tasty meal. Full of protein and fresh in the shops daily, it is the ideal food for families and at the same time can offer some of the chief delights of a Cordon Bleu table.

British fish recipes. are generally very simple; plain grilled or fried fish are our favourites. But continental Europe is a source for hundreds of more elaborate dishes, with exquisite sauces and exciting combinations of different fish. You will find, therefore, that many of the recipes in this book are from the continent.

The specialists in shellfish cooking, though, are the Americans and many of the delicious recipes in our shellfish section are derived from the USA. There is around the Pacific shores an unmatched variety of shellfish and though our shellfish are by no means the same, we can imitate many of the ideas the Americans use to get the best out of this food.

We have selected as wide a variation of recipes as we could, from all kinds of places. If there is anything you don't understand in any of them, there is an appendix of notes and basic recipes for items that recur throughout the book and a glossary of the cooking terms used. We hope that even inexperienced cooks will find enough here to help them through the most complicated recipe. We enjoy all these dishes and would find it hard to pick a favourite. We hope you will try several and, whichever you choose, we wish you success and happy cooking.

Rosemary Hume
Muriel Downes

7

White fish

Whether you go for the delicate Dover sole or the common cod, you can make a luxury of white fish. Choose one of the plainer dishes for a family occasion, or go for a fantastic fish soufflé, a rich mousse or fish cream when you are entertaining special guests.

Many of the dishes in this section are basically poached fish with a sauce. Poaching is carried out in a small quantity of liquid in the oven or on top of the cooker, and the resulting juices are usually added to the sauce. Any fish cooked in this way should be done in court bouillon rather than water, to add flavour to the dish — it is like using a bone stock instead of water for a meat dish. Preparation of this need not be particularly time-consuming either, as the poaching liquid from one lot of fish can be strained and saved for the next if not required for the sauce ; and in any case a court bouillon takes very little time. Alternatively some of the recipes use a fish stock prepared in much the same way as a meat stock.

Whichever way you cook white fish, whether it is poached, grilled, fried or baked, you are sure of a delicate flavour and texture — add a wine or cream sauce and you have one of the prime delicacies of the table.

If you buy fish from a normal town fishmonger, he will certainly do any cleaning and filleting you want. If, however, you are lucky enough to get fish so fresh it hasn't had time to reach the shops, you will need to attend to these jobs yourself. Details of how to do this are on pages 150 and 151 ; you do need a sharp knife though, or you will find the fish breaking up in your hands.

All set to go then? Dinner party or family supper, fish will make the meal.

Fish en coquille

1½ lb firm white fish steak (cod, or
  turbot)
cut lemon, or juice of ½ lemon
salt
½ cucumber
black pepper (ground from mill)
1 teaspoon chopped parsley, mint
  and chives (mixed)
½ teaspoon white wine vinegar
1 tablespoon boiling water
¼ pint thick mayonnaise
6 lettuce leaves
12 anchovy fillets

6 deep scallop shells

Method

First wash the fish. If using cod,
dry it well and rub the surface
with a cut lemon, sprinkle with
salt and leave in a cool place
for 30-60 minutes ; if using turbot,
soak it for 15-20 minutes in cold
water with a little salt and lemon
juice.

Wipe the fish and place it in
a well buttered ovenproof dish,
adding an extra squeeze of
lemon juice, and cover with buttered paper ; poach in a moderate oven at 350°F or Mark 4.
Allow 15-20 minutes depending
on the thickness of the fish.

Peel the cucumber and cut
it into small dice, salt lightly and
leave in a cool place for 30 minutes, then drain away any liquid.
Season the cucumber with black
pepper, add the herbs and
sprinkle with the wine vinegar.
Whisk the boiling water into the
mayonnaise.

Place a lettuce leaf in each
scallop shell and then a spoonful
of prepared cucumber. When
the fish is cold, remove the skin
and bones, then carefully flake
flesh with a fork ; spoon fish
into the shells and coat with the
mayonnaise. Decorate the top
of each shell with anchovy fillets.

1 *Flaking the poached fish ready to
place on the lettuce and cucumber*
2 *Laying the anchovy fillets on
the mayonnaise-coated fish*

Salt cod (morue) louasardaise

2 lb salt cod
$\frac{1}{4}$ pint milk and water (mixed together)
1$\frac{1}{2}$ lb potatoes
$\frac{1}{2}$ oz butter
6 eggs (hard-boiled)
8 oz prawns (shelled)
Parmesan cheese

For béchamel sauce
$\frac{3}{4}$ pint flavoured milk
1$\frac{1}{2}$ oz butter
1$\frac{1}{4}$ oz plain flour
2 tablespoons double cream

For hollandaise sauce
3 tablespoons white wine vinegar
1 slice of onion
3-4 peppercorns
2 egg yolks
3-4 oz butter
salt and pepper

This dish may be made with smoked haddock or fresh cod in place of salt cod.

If using salt cod, soak it for 2-4 hours, changing the water from time to time. This will remove any excess salt.

Method

Set oven at 350°F or Mark 4. Wash and dry the fish, place in ovenproof dish with milk and water and poach in pre-set moderate oven for 30 minutes. Drain fish well and flake, removing skin and bones. Boil the potatoes and cream them with $\frac{1}{2}$ oz butter. Chop the eggs.

Make béchamel sauce in the usual way and finish by stirring in the cream.

To prepare the hollandaise sauce, reduce the vinegar with the onion and peppercorns to 1 dessertspoon. Strain this on to the egg yolks beaten with $\frac{1}{2}$ oz butter. Stand the bowl in a bain-marie over gentle heat and thicken sauce, gradually adding the rest of the butter. When it is ready, beat it into the béchamel sauce and adjust seasoning. Set oven at 450°F or Mark 6.

Layer this sauce with the fish, prawns and chopped eggs in an ovenproof dish, beginning and ending with a layer of sauce. Top with the creamed potato and dust well with Parmesan cheese. Brown in the pre-set quick oven.

Brandade 1

1 lb salt cod, or 1½ lb fresh cod
  fillet
salt (optional)
squeeze of lemon juice (optional)
béchamel sauce (made with
  1 oz butter, ¾ oz flour, ½ pint
  flavoured milk)
7½ fl oz olive oil
½ clove of garlic (lightly crushed)
pepper
little grated nutmeg

For serving
small croûtes of bread fried in
  olive oil, or 11 black, or green,
  olives (stoned)

The classic brandade comes
from the South of France and
is made from salt cod, well
soaked before cooking. The
flesh is then pounded and well
lubricated with good olive oil
and strongly flavoured with
garlic. A less pungent brandade is made from fresh white
fish, which, after cooking, is
pounded in the same way. The
amount of oil added is a little
less and a white or béchamel
sauce is worked in with garlic to
taste.

Method
Soak the salt cod in water for
24 hours and rinse thoroughly
before cooking in water to
cover for 20-30 minutes. If
using fresh cod, wash and dry
it, sprinkle with salt and leave
for 30 minutes. Tip away any
liquid, wipe off the excess salt,
add a squeeze of lemon, cover
with a buttered paper and poach
in the oven for 10-15 minutes
at 350°F or Mark 4.

When the fish is cooked,
drain it very well and pass it
through a mincer or pound
in a mortar until absolutely
smooth.

Watchpoint It is absolutely
essential to break down the
fibres of the fish if the brandade
is to hold the oil and sauce.

Prepare the béchamel sauce
and keep it hot in a bain-marie.
Heat the oil in a small pan, drop
in the garlic and fry it until
yellow, then remove it from the
oil and discard it.

Put the fish in a pan and then
add a little of the hot béchamel
sauce (about 2 tablespoons),
beat well over heat and when
the sauce is absorbed add the
same quantity of the hot oil and
beat again. Continue in this
way until all the sauce and oil is
absorbed and the mixture is as
light and fluffy as a potato
mousseline. Season with pepper
and a very little grated nutmeg.
Serve in a mound on a hot flat
dish and surround with croûtes
(or olives).

Brandade 2

1½ lb fresh cod, or
    haddock, fillet
2-3 drops of lemon juice
2 medium-size potatoes
scant ¼ pint olive oil
1 clove of garlic (lightly crushed)
7½ fl oz béchamel sauce
salt and pepper
5-6 tablespoons hot milk
slices from a French loaf (rubbed
    with garlic and fried in oil) —
    for croûtes

Method
Set oven at 350°F or Mark 4.

Wash and dry the fish and sprinkle with salt ; leave it for 30 minutes, then drain away the liquid and wipe fish well with a cloth. Squeeze over a few drops of lemon juice, cover fish with buttered paper and poach in pre-set oven for 20 minutes, then bone, flake and chop the fish.

Boil potatoes and push through a wire sieve or ricer. Add to the fish and then turn the mixture into a double saucepan.

Heat the oil in a small pan ; fry crushed garlic until it begins to turn yellow. Now beat this oil into fish mixture with the béchamel sauce, adding the seasoning and hot milk, until the mixture is light and creamy. **Watchpoint** The sauce, oil and milk must be added slowly over a gentle heat otherwise the mixture will not absorb liquid completely and it will be impossible to obtain a velvety texture.

Pile brandade into a hot dish and surround with croûtes.

Cod alla napolitana

2 lb fresh cod
½ oz plain flour
oil (for frying)

For tomato sauce
1 tablespoon oil
2 cloves of garlic (chopped)
½ lb tomatoes (sliced)
salt and pepper
1 tablespoon capers
12 black olives (stoned)
pinch of cayenne pepper
1 cap of canned pimiento
    (chopped)

This dish is prepared in Italy with salt cod and served on Good Friday, but in this country fresh cod can be used instead.

Method
Cut the fish from the bone, remove the skin and cut into 2-inch squares. Dust lightly with flour and quickly fry 2-3 pieces at a time until golden-brown in a little hot oil. Drain and put into an ovenproof dish.

Wipe out the pan, add the oil with the cloves of garlic and fry gently for a few seconds until golden-brown. Remove the garlic from the oil, add the tomatoes, season and cook until pulpy. Rub through a strainer and return to the pan with the capers, olives, cayenne and pimiento. Simmer for 2-3 minutes. Spoon this sauce over the cod in the dish, cover with a buttered paper and bake in a moderate oven, 350°F or Mark 4, for 15-20 minutes.

Cod alla romana

2 lb fresh cod
$\frac{1}{2}$ oz plain flour
oil (for frying fish)
3 green peppers
3-4 tablespoons olive oil
2 onions (sliced)
1 lb tomatoes (scalded, skinned,
    seeds removed, flesh roughly
    chopped)
1 tablespoon chopped parsley

This recipe has also been adapted to use fresh, rather than salt, cod.

Method

Cut the fish from the bone, remove the skin and cut flesh into 2-inch pieces. Sprinkle with salt and leave for 30 minutes to draw out the moisture. Tip off any liquid, dry on absorbent paper and roll in a little flour. Fry the fish quickly in a little hot oil until golden-brown, then remove from the pan, drain well and keep on one side.

Cut the green peppers in half, remove the core and seeds and cut flesh into thin strips. Drop the strips into boiling salted water, cook for 1 minute then drain, refresh and drain again. Heat the oil in a large pan, add the onions and cook slowly until golden, then mix in the tomatoes, and cook slowly for about 15 minutes. Then add the green peppers and continue to cook until tender. Add the pieces of fish, simmer for 10 minutes and then serve in a hot dish, sprinkled with the chopped parsley.

Halibut goulart

1½-2 lb halibut steak (about
    ¼ inch thick)
2 eggs
1 tablespoon water, or white
    wine
maize meal
¼ oz plain flour
salt and pepper
5 oz butter
1 clove of garlic (crushed with
    pinch of salt)
4-5 anchovy fillets (pounded)
pinch of paprika pepper
squeeze of lemon juice
1 teaspoon chopped tarragon
½ bunch of watercress (for
    garnish)

This recipe, in which an
especially firm-fibred fish is
necessary, can be made equally
well with turbot.

Method
Wash and dry halibut steak, then
chill thoroughly until it is firm.
Remove the skin and bones,
then cut into strips about 5
inches long and 1½ inches wide.
Beat the eggs with a fork and
mix with the water (or wine).
Dip the pieces of fish in this,
then roll in maize meal, mixed
with flour, salt and pepper.

Heat 2-3 oz butter in a large
pan, put in the fish strips and
sauté until they are lightly-
brown on both sides. Lift strips
on to an ovenproof dish and
keep warm. Add another 2 oz
butter to the pan and, when
bubbling, add the crushed garlic, the pounded anchovies and
the paprika pepper. Add lemon
juice and tarragon. Pour this
mixture over the fish and serve
very hot, garnished with sprigs
of watercress.

Sweet and sour halibut

4 halibut steaks
1 medium-size onion (sliced)
1 medium-size carrot (peeled and sliced)
$\frac{1}{2}$-$\frac{3}{4}$ pint water
2-3 strips of lemon rind
salt and pepper
1 oz granulated sugar
juice of 2 lemons
2 eggs (beaten)
chopped parsley (to garnish)

Method
Boil the onion and carrot in the water for 10 minutes. Add lemon rind, seasoning, sugar and lemon juice. Place the fish steaks in this pan and poach for 20-30 minutes, or transfer to an oven-proof dish and cook gently in the middle of a moderate oven, pre-set at 350°F or Mark 4, for the same length of time.

Lift out the fish steaks, drain them well and place in a serving dish. Strain cooking liquid and cool ; add beaten eggs and heat this sauce gently until it thickens, stirring continuously and taking care not to curdle it by overheating. Allow sauce to cool. Pour a little sauce over and around the fish and hand the remainder separately. Garnish dish with chopped parsley and serve cold with peas and carrots.

Halibut Pondicherry

1$\frac{1}{2}$-2 lb halibut steaks
1 wineglass white wine
1 wineglass water
6-8 peppercorns
few drops of lemon juice
2 Spanish onions (sliced, blanched and cooked in butter)

For sauce
1 oz butter
1 shallot (chopped)
1 teaspoon curry powder
1 oz plain flour
$\frac{1}{4}$ pint milk
2$\frac{1}{2}$ fl oz single cream

Method
Set oven at 350°F or Mark 4. Place the fish in a buttered ovenproof dish, pour over the wine and water, surround with peppercorns and squeeze over a few drops of lemon juice. Cover with a buttered paper and poach in pre-set oven for 20-30 minutes. Pour off the stock, strain it and set aside. Skin the fish, removing the bone, and keep it warm.

To make the sauce : melt the 1 oz butter in a saucepan, add the shallot and after a minute or so stir in the curry powder. Cook gently for 30 seconds, stir in the flour and then the strained liquor from the fish. Thicken over heat, then add the milk. Bring to boil, simmer for 3-4 minutes, then add cream.

Arrange the prepared Spanish onions on the serving dish and put fish on top ; coat with sauce.

Halibut bergère

4-5 halibut steaks
1 onion
4-6 oz mushrooms
2 wineglasses white wine
1 wineglass water
salt and pepper
3 thin slices of stale bread
butter (for frying)
chopped parsley

For hollandaise sauce
2 tablespoons tarragon vinegar
1 slice of onion
6 peppercorns
1 blade of mace
1 egg yolk (beaten)
2 oz butter

For velouté sauce
$1\frac{1}{4}$ oz butter
1 oz plain flour
$\frac{1}{2}-\frac{3}{4}$ pint stock (from the fish)
2-3 tablespoons double cream

Method
Wash and dry the fish steaks. Set oven at 300-325°F or Mark 2-3. Chop the onion very finely ; wash and chop mushrooms. Thickly butter an oven-proof dish, scatter the mixture down the centre and place the fish on the top. Pour over the wine and water and season lightly. Cover with buttered paper and poach in a pre-set moderately slow oven for 20-25 minutes.

Meanwhile prepare hollandaise sauce : put vinegar and flavourings in a pan and reduce quantity by half. Cream the egg yolk with $\frac{1}{4}$ oz butter ; strain and add the liquid. Thicken sauce in a bain-marie, gradually adding the remaining butter. When thick, cover bowl with grease-proof paper and set aside.

Cut bread carefully in julienne strips (this cutting improves the appearance of the finished dish), and fry until golden-brown in butter ; set aside.

To make velouté sauce : melt $1\frac{1}{4}$ oz butter in a pan, blend in the flour and cook to a pale straw colour. Strain on fish liquor, blend and thicken sauce over heat, add cream and simmer until it is syrupy.

Adjust the seasoning and beat in hollandaise sauce off the heat. Dish up the fish with the dux-elles (onion and mushroom mixture), coat with the sauce and glaze under the grill. Scatter over or surround the dish with the julienne bread and sprinkle with chopped parsley.

Halibut dieppoise

1½ lb halibut steak
salt and pepper
juice of ½ lemon
2 oz butter

For salpicon
2 leeks
1 oz butter
1 teaspoon paprika pepper
4 oz prawns (shelled)
black pepper

Method

Set oven at 350°F or Mark 4. Wash and dry the fish, place it in an ovenproof dish, season and add lemon juice. Melt the 2 oz butter and pour it over the fish ; cover and cook in pre-set moderate oven for about 20 minutes. Baste from time to time.

Meanwhile slice the white part of the leek in rounds, soften in the butter, add the paprika and prawns and heat gently. Shred the green of the leeks and blanch for 2-3 minutes ; drain and refresh and add to the pan. Season with black pepper.

Take up the fish carefully, remove the bone and skin and spoon the salpicon over the top.

Halibut dieppoise has a salpicon of prawns and leeks seasoned with paprika and black pepper

Quenelles de brochet

1 lb halibut or turbot steak
¾ lb whiting fillet
3 eggs
1½ oz butter (creamed)
mushroom, or Nantua, sauce

For panade
¼ pint water
¼ pint milk
2 oz butter
salt and pepper
5 oz plain flour (sifted twice
   with ½ teaspoon salt)

'Brochet' is French for pike, a fish common to rivers in France. As pike is not readily available here, we suggest halibut, or turbot, as alternatives.

Method
Skin and mince the fish, then weigh. The turbot (or halibut) should weigh 10 oz ; the whiting 7 oz.

To prepare the panade : bring the water, milk and butter to the boil with the seasoning. Have the flour ready. When the liquid comes to the boil draw off the heat and at once shoot in all the flour. Beat until smooth. Turn out and allow to get quite cold.

Watchpoint Check here by weighing the panade and the combined fish ; they should be equal in weight.

Pound the fish thoroughly, then gradually add the panade, working it well. Add the eggs, one at a time, and the butter. Season and chill overnight.

Watchpoint Once the eggs have been added the mixture will be quite soft, but with the chilling overnight it will be stiff enough to handle.

When ready to cook, divide the mixture into 6-8 even portions, roll lightly to a thick sausage, then carefully drop in the boiling salted water and poach for 18-20 minutes. Then lift out with the draining spoon, touching the bowl of the spoon on a piece of absorbent paper to remove any moisture. Put into a buttered shallow gratin dish and coat with a creamy mushroom sauce. Put into a moderate oven at 350°F or Mark 4 for about 5 minutes to make sure the quenelles are thoroughly hot. Serve at once.

Plaice gratiné

2 plaice (each weighing 2 lb)
1 large raw potato
2-3 tablespoons oil, or butter
1 handful fresh breadcrumbs
1 wineglass white wine
1 wineglass water
salt
6 peppercorns
bayleaf
blade of mace
$\frac{1}{2}$ oz butter
2 shallots (chopped)
3-4 oz mushrooms (chopped)
1 dessertspoon chopped parsley

For sauce
1 oz butter
$\frac{3}{4}$ oz plain flour
5 fl oz top of milk, or single cream

Method
Grate the potato coarsely and soak in cold water for half an hour, drain and dry well. Separate the flakes with a fork. Fry in the oil (or butter) until crisp, then remove and fry the crumbs in the same way ; keep both warm.

Set oven at 350°F or Mark 4. Skin the fillets, wash, dry and fold them. Lay in a buttered ovenproof dish, pour over the wine and water, add seasoning, bayleaf and mace.

Poach in pre-set oven for 10 minutes. Melt $\frac{1}{2}$ oz butter in a pan, add shallot and, after a few minutes, the mushrooms. Cook for 3-4 minutes, season well and add parsley.

Pour off liquor from the fish. Make a roux with the 1 oz butter and flour, add the liquor, stir until thickening, then add milk (or cream). Boil and then simmer for a few minutes. Serve fillets on mushroom mixture, coated with sauce and scattered with crumbs and potato.

Fish cream Newburg

1 lb fresh haddock fillet (skinned and minced)
2 eggs (beaten)
$2\frac{1}{2}$ fl oz double cream

For panade
$7\frac{1}{2}$ fl oz milk
2 oz butter
$2\frac{1}{2}$ oz plain flour
salt and pepper

For sauce
1 oz butter
$\frac{1}{2}$ teaspoon paprika pepper
$\frac{3}{4}$ oz plain flour
$7\frac{1}{2}$ fl oz fish stock
    (see page 60)
1 small can lobster meat, or prawns
$\frac{1}{2}$ glass sherry
$2\frac{1}{2}$ fl oz double cream

7-inch diameter cake tin, or 8-8$\frac{1}{2}$ inch diameter savarin mould

Method
First make the panade : bring the milk to the boil with the butter, draw pan aside, add the flour all at once and beat until smooth. Season panade and allow to cool.

Pound the fish with the panade, or work it in a blender, and add the beaten eggs and cream. Adjust the seasoning. Fill cream into the buttered tin or mould, cover with buttered paper and foil, then steam or poach cream au bain-marie for about 40 minutes or until firm to the touch.

Meanwhile prepare the sauce : melt the butter, add the paprika to pan and cook gently for 1 minute. Stir in the flour and continue cooking until it is marbled. Draw pan aside and blend in the stock. Return pan

to the heat and stir until sauce is boiling. Heat the lobster meat (or prawns) in the sherry and add to the sauce with the cream.

Adjust the seasoning.

Turn the cream on to a hot serving dish and spoon over the sauce.

Seafood and watercress cocktail

For fish mousse
12 oz fresh haddock fillet
salt and pepper
juice of ½ lemon
¼ pint cold white sauce (made
with ½ oz butter, ½ oz flour
and ¼ pint milk)
1 packet (about 2 oz) Demi-Sel
cream cheese
1 tablespoon snipped chives
about 2 tablespoons finely
chopped watercress stalks
2-3 tablespoons double cream

For prawn mixture
¾ pint (6-8 oz) prawns (shelled)
½ teaspoon paprika pepper
1 tablespoon tomato chutney,
or ketchup
½ pint mayonnaise
4 tablespoons chopped celery
1 teaspoon horseradish cream

Method

Set oven at 350°F or Mark 4.

First prepare the fish mousse. Season the haddock fillet, squeeze over the lemon juice and bake in pre-set oven for about 15 minutes. When cool, flake the fish and crush with a fork. Beat in the white sauce and Demi-Sel cheese ; when quite smooth, add the chives and watercress stalks and season to taste.

Watchpoint The watercress stalks should be very finely chopped and enough should be added to give the fish mousse a pleasant green colour and a peppery flavour, so increase the quantity to suit your personal taste. Remember that the watercress stalks must be stripped of every tiny leaf.

Stir in just enough cream to give a dropping consistency. Keep mousse on one side.

Add the paprika and tomato chutney (or ketchup) to the mayonnaise ; season to taste, then add the chopped celery and horseradish cream. Fold in the prawns. Place the prawn mixture and fish mousse in alternate layers in wine goblets, or sundae glasses, starting and finishing with the prawn mixture.

White sauce

¾ oz butter
1 rounded tablespoon plain flour
½ pint milk
salt and pepper

Method

Melt the butter in a pan, remove from heat and stir in the flour. Blend in half the milk, then stir in the rest. Stir over moderate heat until boiling, then boil gently for 1-2 minutes. Season to taste.

Suprêmes of fish parisienne

$\frac{3}{4}$ lb haddock, or hake
2 small egg whites
6 fl oz double cream
salt and pepper

For salpicon
3 oz button mushrooms (thinly sliced)
scant $\frac{1}{2}$ oz butter
1 tablespoon strained fish stock, or sherry

For suprême sauce
1$\frac{1}{4}$ oz butter
1 oz plain flour
7$\frac{1}{2}$ fl oz strong fish stock
2 egg yolks
4 fl oz single cream

6-8 cutlet moulds, or deep tartlet tins

This recipe can also be done with white meat such as minced chicken. If you use chicken, some shredded cooked ham may be added to the mushrooms in the salpicon. If wished, this dish can be garnished with sauté button mushrooms (champignons de Paris) from which it gets the name, parisienne.

Method
Skin and mince the fish, then weigh — there should be $\frac{1}{2}$ lb. Break the egg whites slightly with a fork, then gradually beat into the fish. Pass the mixture through a wire sieve, or work in a blender. Return it to the bowl and add the cream gradually and season as soon as cream has all been added. Set aside. Butter the moulds (or tins) well. Sauté the mushrooms quickly for 1-2 minutes in the butter, add the fish stock (or sherry) and season. Fill moulds (or tins) with the mousse and level off the tops with a knife. Dip your little finger, or the bowl of a teaspoon, into a little egg white and then use to make a hole in the top of each little suprême. Fill the mushroom salpicon into the hollows just formed, then cover completely with the mousse. Again level the tops with a palette knife.

Have ready a sauté or stewpan three-quarters filled with boiling salted water. Drop the moulds into the water and poach for 8-10 minutes. Meanwhile prepare the suprême sauce : melt the butter in a pan, stir in the flour and cook to a pale straw colour. Blend in the fish stock, bring to the boil and simmer until sauce begins to thicken. Mix together egg yolks and cream ; add a tablespoon of hot sauce and stir this liaison into the sauce.

During the poaching give the handle of the pan a slight shake once or twice. This will cause the suprêmes to detach themselves from the moulds and float to the surface of the water. This indicates that they are done, so lift out carefully with a draining spoon or fish slice and tip on to a cloth or piece of absorbent paper. For serving arrange them on a dish and coat with the suprême sauce.

Watchpoint Dariole moulds can be used in place of cutlet or tartlet moulds, but if they are used, the fish suprêmes must be steamed or cooked au bain-marie and then turned out.

Fresh haddock mousse

1 lb fresh haddock fillet
salt
6 peppercorns
lemon juice

For mousse
½ pint milk
1 slice of onion
1 bayleaf
6 peppercorns
1 oz butter
1 teaspoon paprika pepper
¾ oz plain flour
1 dessertspoon gelatine (soaked in
   3-4 tablespoons water)
3 tablespoons double cream
1 egg white

To finish
¼ pint mayonnaise
1-2 tablespoons tomato juice
   (canned)
dash of Tabasco sauce
slices of tomato, or cucumber

Plain, or fish-shaped, mould (1½
   pints capacity)

Method
Set oven at 350°F or Mark 4.

Wash and skin the fillet and place it in a buttered ovenproof dish with the seasoning and lemon juice. Cover dish with a buttered paper and cook, in pre-set moderate oven, for about 12-15 minutes. Allow fish to cool. Oil the mould lightly.

To prepare mousse : heat the milk with the onion, bayleaf and peppercorns, and infuse until it is well flavoured, then strain. Melt the butter, add the paprika pepper and cook for 1 minute ; remove pan from the heat, blend in the flour and the strained milk. Stir sauce until it is boiling, then tip it into a bowl ; cover and allow to cool.

Strain the fish and pound it in a bowl, adding cold sauce a little at a time. Dissolve gelatine over gentle heat, add to fish mixture.

Lightly whip the cream and stiffly whisk the egg white. Fold these into the fish mixture, turn into mould, leave to set.

Turn out mousse on to a serving dish. Coat with the mayonnaise, thinned slightly with the tomato juice and flavoured with Tabasco sauce. Garnish with slices of tomato or cucumber.

Turning the haddock mousse into the fish mould before leaving it to set

Smoked haddock mousse

8 oz smoked haddock (weighed when cooked and flaked — allow 1 lb on the bone, or $\frac{3}{4}$ lb fillet)
2 eggs (hard-boiled)
$\frac{1}{2}$ int cold béchamel sauce
$\frac{1}{4}$ pint mayonnaise
$\frac{1}{4}$ oz gelatine
2$\frac{1}{2}$ fl oz chicken stock, or water
2$\frac{1}{2}$ fl oz double cream (lightly whipped)

To finish
2 eggs (hard-boiled)
$\frac{1}{2}$-$\frac{3}{4}$ pint aspic jelly (see page 58)

6-inch diameter top (No. 2 size) soufflé dish

Method

Have the haddock ready-cooked and flaked and the eggs chopped. Mix the béchamel sauce and mayonnaise together. Soak the gelatine in the stock (or water), dissolve it over gentle heat and add to the sauce mixture. Stir in the haddock and eggs and, as the mixture begins to thicken, fold in the cream. Turn into the soufflé dish until about three-quarters full, cover mousse and leave it to set in a cool place.

When set, decorate the top with thin slices of hard-boiled eggs and enough cool aspic to cover ; leave to set. Fill the dish with more aspic and leave again to set before serving the mousse.

Haddock dieppoise

1-1$\frac{1}{2}$ lb haddock fillet (skinned)
butter
lemon juice
3 pints of mussels
1 small onion (quartered)
1 wineglass white wine
$\frac{1}{2}$ wineglass water
4 oz shrimps or prawns (shelled)
1 rounded tablespoon grated cheese

For sauce
1 oz butter
$\frac{1}{2}$ oz plain flour
$\frac{1}{2}$ pint mussel liquor
5 tablespoons creamy milk

Method

Cut fillet into portions, put in a well buttered ovenproof dish, squeeze over a little lemon juice and cover with buttered paper. Poach in the oven at 350°F or Mark 4 for 15 minutes.

To prepare mussels : well scrub mussels make sure that all are tightly closed and put into a pan. Add the onion, wine and water. Cover and bring to the boil, shaking pan occasionally. When mussels are well opened, remove from shells and take off the beards. Set mussels aside, strain and measure the liquor.

To prepare sauce : make roux, then pour in $\frac{1}{2}$ pint mussel liquor and stir until boiling. Add milk and boil for 2-3 minutes.

Dish up the haddock, scatter the mussels and shrimps over the top, and coat with the sauce. Sprinkle cheese over the top and brown under the grill.

1 The skinned haddock being cut into portions and placed in a dish for haddock dieppoise
2 The mussels and shrimps being scattered over cooked haddock before coating it with sauce

The finished haddock dieppoise

29

Fish croquettes

1 lb fresh haddock fillet
salt and pepper
juice of ¼ lemon
½ pint milk (infused with 1
   slice of onion, 1 blade of
   mace, ½ bayleaf, 6 peppercorns)
1½ oz butter
1½ oz plain flour
1 rounded teaspoon gelatine
   (soaked in 1 tablespoon cold
   water)
1 egg (beaten)

For frying
2-3 tablespoons seasoned flour
1 egg (beaten)
dried white breadcrumbs
bunch of parsley (well washed
   and dried) — to garnish

Deep fat bath or pan, and basket ;
square cake tin, or oval pie dish

Method

Wash and dry the fish, place in a buttered, ovenproof dish, season and add a squeeze of lemon juice. Cover with buttered paper and cook for 10-12 minutes in the oven at 325°F or Mark 3.

Infuse the milk with the flavourings in a pan, then strain and set aside to cool. Meanwhile flake the fish, removing the skin and bones.

Melt the butter in a small saucepan, stir in the flour, remove from the heat and blend in the strained milk, beating well to avoid lumps. Season and stir over a gentle heat until boiling ; then simmer for 1 minute. Add the flaked fish a little at a time, beating the mixture well. This breaks the fibres of the fish and helps the mixture to bind. Add the soaked gelatine to the hot fish mixture, stir until dissolved and well distributed. (The small quantity of gelatine is not detected when the croquettes are served hot, but makes the mixture much easier to handle when cold.)

Add the beaten egg and taste for seasoning. Turn mixture into a square cake tin or oval pie dish and leave to cool. Then place in refrigerator until really chilled and firm. Cut into strips about 3 inches long and 1 inch wide and deep. Roll them with two palette knives into neat cork-shaped croquettes on a floured board. Use as little seasoned flour as possible and avoid working it into the fish mixture. Brush each croquette with beaten egg and roll in the breadcrumbs. Heat the fat or oil to 375°F.

Watchpoint Before you start frying, make absolutely sure that you have enough fat in the pan to cover the croquettes.

Fry the croquettes until golden-brown, drain well, then turn carefully on to absorbent paper. Turn the heat off and leave the fat 2-3 minutes to cool a little. Put the parsley in the fat basket and lower it very gently into the fat ; don't immerse it until the violent spluttering stops. When the bubbling stops, drain the parsley well ; it should still be bright green and very crisp.

Serve the croquettes with Dutch sauce (see right).

1 *When chilled and firm, cut fish mixture into long strips*

2 *Roll it into small cork-shaped croquettes on a floured board, using two palette knives*

3 *Brush the croquettes with a little beaten egg before rolling them in the dried breadcrumbs*

4 *When frying croquettes make sure that the fat covers them to seal the coating, otherwise they are very likely to burst*

Dutch sauce

$\frac{3}{4}$ **pint milk (infused with 1 slice of onion, $\frac{1}{2}$ bayleaf, 6 peppercorns)**
$1\frac{1}{2}$ oz butter
$1\frac{1}{4}$ oz plain flour
salt
2 egg yolks
juice of $\frac{1}{2}$ lemon

Method

Infuse the milk with the flavourings, then strain into a bowl.

Melt the butter in a small saucepan, remove from the heat and blend in the flour and strained milk. Add salt to taste and stir mixture over a gentle heat until boiling. Simmer for 1-2 minutes.

Draw pan away from the heat, allow to cool very slightly then beat in the egg yolks. Reheat without boiling and add the lemon juice. Taste for seasoning. Use immediately.

Fish croquettes vert-pré

1 lb fresh haddock fillet
salt and pepper
6 peppercorns
squeeze of lemon juice
2 tablespoons water
½ lb potatoes
1 bunch of watercress
1 oz butter
1 egg
bunch of parsley (well washed
   and dried) — to garnish

For coating croquettes
2 tablespoons seasoned flour
1 egg (beaten)
dried white breadcrumbs

Deep fat bath

Method
Wash the haddock, then place in a lightly buttered ovenproof dish. Season with salt, add the peppercorns, lemon juice and water. Cover with a buttered paper and poach fish in a moderate oven, pre-set at 350°F or Mark 4, for 12-15 minutes. Drain fish, then flake and crush with a fork.

Peel and quarter the potatoes ; wash the watercress well ; cook both together in a pan of boiling, salted water until the potatoes are just tender. Drain well, dry both over gentle heat, then pass through a sieve.

Mix the fish and potato and watercress purée together, add the butter, season to taste, add egg and beat well. Form mixture into croquettes, using a palette knife to shape the ends. Roll the croquettes in seasoned flour, coat with beaten egg and white crumbs. Fry croquettes in deep fat until golden-brown (about 3 minutes) then drain on absorbent paper. Turn the heat off and leave the fat 2-3 minutes to cool

a little. Put the parsley in the fat basket and lower it very gently into the fat ; don't immerse it until the spluttering stops. When the bubbling stops, drain the parsley well. Serve the croquettes garnished with fried parsley and the tartare sauce separately.

Tartare sauce

2 eggs (hard-boiled)
1 egg yolk (raw)
salt and pepper
½ pint oil
1 tablespoon vinegar
1 teaspoon chopped parsley
1 teaspoon snipped chives
1 teaspoon chopped capers, or
   gherkins

Method
Cut the hard-boiled eggs in half, remove the yolks and rub them through a strainer into a bowl. Add the raw yolk and seasoning ; work well together. Add the oil drop by drop, as for a mayonnaise, and dilute with the vinegar as necessary. Finish off with the herbs and capers. If wished, add the shredded white of one of the hard-boiled eggs.

Smoked haddock roulade

8 oz (2 cups) smoked haddock
  (cooked and flaked)
4 eggs
3 rounded tablespoons dry
  cheese (grated)

For filling
béchamel sauce made with 1½ oz
  butter, ¾ oz flour, ¾ pint flavoured,
  or plain, milk.
salt and pepper
1 dessertspoon anchovy essence
3 eggs (hard-boiled and finely
  chopped)

*Swiss roll tin (12 inches by 8 inches),
  or baking sheet with a raised edge*

Tunny fish, canned or fresh
salmon or crab meat may be
used in this dish.

*Smoked haddock roulade : prepare
fish, filling and sauce, mix a little
sauce with fish and beat in yolks
and cheese*

Method

First prepare the filling : make
béchamel sauce, season and
add anchovy essence. The
sauce should be creamy and
thick enough just to drop from
the spoon.

Take 3 tablespoons of sauce
and add to the cooked fish.
Add the chopped eggs to the
remaining sauce ; cover and set
aside but keep warm.

Grease tin or baking sheet
well. Line with greaseproof
paper and grease again. Set
oven at 400°F or Mark 6.

Separate eggs and beat yolks
into the fish with one-third of
the cheese. Whip whites to a
firm snow and cut and fold into
fish mixture, with a metal spoon.

Put on to the tin and spread
evenly. Bake on top shelf of

*Having stirred egg whites into fish
mixture, spread evenly over the
case set on a greased baking sheet.
Bake in the oven until firm*

pre-set oven for 10-15 minutes or until well risen and firm to the touch.

Have ready a large sheet of greaseproof paper, sprinkled with the remaining cheese. Quickly turn the roulade on to this, strip off the paper it was cooked on and spread roulade with the filling. Trim off sides, then tilt paper and roll up mixture in the same way as for a swiss roll (see photograph, far right). Put on to a hot serving dish and sprinkle with additional cheese, if wished.

Turn cooked roulade on to grease-proof paper sprinkled with cheese ; spread filling over roulade, trim sides, tilt paper and roll up

Brill Durand

2-2½ lb brill (filleted)
1 wineglass white wine
squeeze of lemon juice
¼ pint single cream, or ¼ pint
   milk and ½ oz kneaded butter
chopped parsley

For vegetable garnish
1 lb carrots
1 lb turnips
½ lb onions
½ oz butter
1 wineglass white wine
bouquet garni
salt and pepper
6 tomatoes (skinned, seeds
   removed, and shredded)

Method

Set oven at 350°F or Mark 4.
Skin the fish, trim, fold fillets
and place in a buttered ovenproof dish with the wine and
lemon juice ; cover with a
buttered paper and poach in
pre-set oven for about 10-12
minutes.

Slice the root vegetables and
place in a shallow pan with
the butter, wine, bouquet garni
and seasoning, cover with a
paper and lid and cook until the
liquid is absorbed and the
vegetables quite tender. Do not
allow to colour. Remove the
bouquet garni, add the tomatoes
and heat carefully.

When the fish is cooked,
strain the liquor from the dish
into a small pan and reduce by
half. Add the cream slowly
(or add milk and kneaded
butter), season well and bring
to the boil. Add the parsley.

Place the vegetables on a hot
serving dish. Arrange the fish
on top and spoon over sauce.

Red mullet with fennel and lemon

4 red mullet (cleaned)
salt
pepper (ground from mill)
4 tablespoons oil, or melted
   butter
1 shallot (finely chopped)
2 heads of Florence fennel
   (finocchio)
1 lemon
1 oz butter
chopped parsley

Method

Trim the mullet and make 3-4
diagonal slits on each side of
fish. Season and marinate in
oil or butter and shallot while
preparing fennel.

Cut fennel into thick slices
and blanch 2-3 minutes ; drain
well. Remove peel and pith
from lemon and cut flesh into
segments. Sauté fennel in butter
until just tender, season and
add lemon and parsley.

Brush grill rack with oil and
pre-heat grill. Remove mullet
from marinade and grill for
8-10 minutes, brushing with
oil if necessary during cooking.
Serve with fennel and lemon
on a hot dish.

I'a (Oven-steamed fish with sweet potatoes)

1 grey mullet (1½-2 lb)
salt and pepper
juice of ½ lemon

Locally caught fish is used for this dish in Fiji. Sometimes 3-4 small fish are used, or one large fish. If you are attempting this dish at home, a firm-fleshed fish such as grey mullet would be suitable. In Fiji the small fish are wrapped in the corn husks but greaseproof paper is quite satisfactory.

Method

Wash and trim the grey mullet, season and squeeze on the lemon juice. Wrap in grease-proof paper and tie up with string. Pour boiling water into the bottom of a roasting tin, set a wire rack over the pan and set the fish on it. Cover and cook in the oven, set at 350°F or Mark 4, until the fish is tender (about 30 minutes).

For serving, remove the paper very carefully and slide fish on to a hot dish with all the juices. Serve with melted butter and fried sweet potatoes.

Note : sweet potatoes are imported and sold in Great Britain wherever immigrants from warmer parts of the Commonwealth live. These tubers — with their tender, sweet flesh — require cool, dry storage at about 55°F. Sweet potatoes may be cooked in most of the ways used for ordinary potatoes. Canned sweet potatoes are sometimes available.

A grey mullet — steamed in the oven in the Fijian style — is garnished with watercress and served with fried sweet potatoes

Whiting soufflé

1 lb whiting (filleted)
3 egg yolks
salt and pepper
pinch of ground mace
1 tablespoon double cream
4 egg whites
2 tablespoons browned crumbs

For béchamel sauce
$\frac{1}{2}$ oz butter
scant $\frac{1}{2}$ oz plain flour
$\frac{1}{4}$ pint flavoured milk

*7-inch diameter top (size No. 1)
soufflé dish*

Method
Tie a doubled band of grease-
proof paper round the soufflé
dish, to stand 3 inches above
the rim. Grease dish and paper
and dust with 1 tablespoon
browned crumbs. Set oven at
375°F or Mark 5.
   Fillet the whiting, remove
skin and bone, and shred flesh
finely.
   Prepare the béchamel sauce.
   Place fish in a mortar or
bowl, add cold béchamel sauce
a little at a time and pound
mixture well. Beat in egg yolks
one at a time. Then rub mixture
through a wire sieve or work in
a blender until smooth and
velvety. Season, add mace and
stir in cream.
   Whisk the egg whites until
stiff and then, using a metal
spoon, stir 1 tablespoon into the
mixture to soften it ; then quickly
and lightly stir in the rest. Turn
at once into prepared soufflé
dish and dust top with browned
crumbs. Bake for 25-30 minutes
in pre-set oven until firm and
evenly-brown.

Fritto misto

For fish croquettes
$1\frac{1}{4}$ lb sole (filleted)
$\frac{1}{2}$ lb white fish (cooked and flaked)
$\frac{1}{2}$ lb scampi
$7\frac{1}{2}$ fl oz milk
1 slice of onion
1 blade of mace
1 bayleaf
6 peppercorns
$1\frac{1}{2}$ oz butter
$1\frac{1}{2}$ oz plain flour
salt and pepper
seasoned flour
1 egg
beaten egg and dried white
   breadcrumbs (for coating)

For fritter batter
3 oz plain flour
pinch of salt
$\frac{1}{4}$ oz yeast
$\frac{1}{4}$-$\frac{1}{2}$ cup warm water
1 tablespoon corn oil

For serving
fried parsley (see method, page 30)
lemon wedges
brown bread and butter
$\frac{1}{2}$ pint Alabama sauce (see page 131)

Deep fat bath

Method
First prepare the fritter batter.
Sift the flour with a pinch of salt,
melt the yeast in the warm water
and stir into the flour to give a
smooth, thick cream. Mix in the
oil and leave batter in a warm
place for 30-40 minutes.
   Now prepare the fish croquette mixture. Infuse the milk
with the onion, mace, bayleaf,
and peppercorns. Melt the
butter, remove pan from the
heat, add the flour and strain
on the milk. Blend until smooth,
season and return pan to the
heat. Stir until boiling. Simmer
for 1-2 minutes, add the flaked

white fish gradually, beating well. Adjust seasoning and beat in the egg. Turn mixture on to a plate and allow to cool.

Shape mixture into small neat cakes, roll in seasoned flour, brush with egg and coat with breadcrumbs.

Cut each fillet of sole into small finger-like pieces, roll in seasoned flour and coat with egg and crumbs. Roll the scampi in seasoned flour and then dip in the fritter batter.

Have the deep fat hot and fry the prepared fish. Pile croquettes into the serving dish and garnish with fried parsley. Hand lemon fingers, brown bread and butter and Alabama sauce separately.

This fritto misto, with Alabama sauce, includes sole and scampi

Carbonade of skate

2 lb skate
salt and pepper
lemon juice
4 oz butter
1 egg (beaten)
dry white breadcrumbs
watercress (to garnish)

Method

Set oven at 425°F or Mark 7. Trim, wash and dry the fish. Cut it into large pieces, season well and sprinkle with lemon juice. Melt half the butter, draw the pieces of skate through this, then through the beaten egg. Roll fish in the crumbs, pressing them well on, and put pieces in a roasting tin or ovenproof dish. Melt the rest of the butter, pour it over the fish and cook in pre-set hot oven for about 15-20 minutes. Serve garnished with the cress and hollandaise sauce (see page 13), or tomato ice, handed separately.

Tomato ice

$\frac{1}{2}$ pint thick mayonnaise
$\frac{1}{2}$ pint tomato pulp (made from 1 lb tomatoes stewed with a little garlic, bayleaf, and lemon thyme or basil to extract juice, and then sieved)
1 teaspoon tomato purée (optional)
juice of 1 large lemon
grated rind of 1 orange
$2\frac{1}{2}$ fl oz double cream (partially whipped)
good pinch of granulated sugar
salt and pepper

Method

Make mayonnaise, using lemon juice instead of vinegar to sharpen. Then incorporate other ingredients in the order given.

Taste mixture and adjust seasoning. Pour it into container and freeze.

As this is a thick and creamy mixture, it is particularly good for freezing in the ice-making compartment of the refrigerator. **Note :** the tomato purée is added if the fresh tomatoes are poor in flavour or lacking in strength.

Gefillte fish

In Jewish households gefillte fish is served often throughout the year, but is also a Passover favourite. The fish used in the basic mixture should be a selection of 3-4 varieties (eg. cod, haddock, halibut, bream, carp, whiting) to give a total weight of 2 lb. There are three methods of serving this chopped fish mixture — either boiled, or fried, or stuffed into a whole fish skin — recipes for which are given after the basic mixture.

Basic gefillte fish

2 lb fish (skinned and filleted ; skin
    and bone are reserved for fish
    stock)
2 onions
1 egg (beaten)
salt
black pepper (ground from mill)
3 tablespoons matzo meal

Method
Mince the fish and onions. Add the beaten egg and season well. Add matzo meal and mix well.

Fried gefillte fish

basic gefillte fish mixture
plain flour
oil (for frying)

To garnish
tomato slices
watercress

Method
Form the basic mixture into flat cakes $\frac{3}{4}$ inch thick and 2 inches in diameter. Roll in flour and fry the cakes in shallow hot oil until they are a deep golden-brown on both sides. Drain them well on absorbent paper. Serve cold, garnished with tomato and watercress.

Boiled gefillte fish

basic gefillte fish mixture

For fish stock
2 onions
2 carrots
1-1$\frac{1}{2}$ pints water
bones and skin of fish
1 teaspoon salt
large pinch of pepper

Method
Roll the basic mixture into balls, measuring about 2 inches in diameter ; make sure your hands are damp so that the mixture does not stick to them.

Slice one onion and one carrot, place in a pan with the water and bones and skin of fish ; season. Bring liquid to the boil and simmer for 20 minutes, then strain this fish stock.

Slice the remaining onion, put into a large pan, or fish kettle, with the second carrot, also sliced. Gently place the fish balls on the bed of vegetables and pour in the fish stock at the side of the pan (to avoid breaking the fish balls). Simmer them very gently for 1-2 hours, until firm to the touch.

Lift fish balls out gently and allow them to cool. Strain the liquid and reserve carrot slices. Serve cold, on a bed of lettuce, placing a carrot slice on each fish ball. Serve the cooking liquid separately in a sauce boat.

Stuffed gefillte fish

1 carp (3-4 lb)

For fish stock
1 onion (sliced)
salt
8 peppercorns
2 pints water
stalk of parsley

For stuffing
1 medium-size onion
2 eggs (hard-boiled)
1 tablespoon sugar
white pepper
2 tablespoons oil
2 eggs (beaten)

For cooking
2 onions (sliced)
2 carrots (sliced)
$\frac{1}{2}$ stick of celery (sliced)

To garnish
chopped aspic (made from
    cooking liquid) — see page 58
bouquets of watercress

This is a rich recipe, especially
suited to a festive occasion.

Method

To remove the flesh and bone
from the fish, leaving the skin
intact : bend the head of the
fish back from the base of the
head and, using a very sharp
knife, work skin away from the
flesh. Gently work from head to
tail, keeping the head attached
to the skin. Then snip bone off
at head and tail with scissors.
Remove flesh from the fish skin.

Put the carp bones and fish
stock ingredients in a pan and
simmer for 20 minutes. Strain
the liquid and reserve.

To prepare stuffing : mince
the carp flesh, onion and hard-
boiled eggs, and mix well. Add
sugar and seasoning and slowly
work in the oil and enough
beaten egg to bind stuffing
together. (If eggs are large you
may not need to use more than
one.) Taking care not to break
fish skin, fill it with stuffing.

Place the onions, carrots and
celery in a fish kettle with the
reserved fish stock. Place the
stuffed fish on the vegetables
and poach for $1\frac{1}{2}$ hours.

Serve the stuffed fish cold,
garnished with chopped aspic
and bouquets of watercress and
accompanied by chrane.

Chrane

Grate or mince 12 oz cooked
beetroot and mix it with 6
tablespoons freshly grated
horseradish, $\frac{3}{4}$ pint white wine
vinegar, 1 teaspoon salt and a
pinch of pepper. Fill in to clean
jars and seal ; keep for 1 week
before using, to develop flavour.

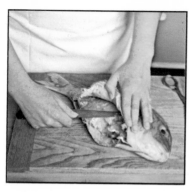

Removing flesh and bone from carp leaving the skin intact

Filling the carp skin with stuffing made of the carp flesh

Matelote mâconnaise

good mixture of fish such as :
  1 lb rock salmon
  2 turbot steaks (each weighing 6 oz)
  4 scallops
3 oz butter
1 onion (finely chopped)
2 wineglasses red wine
½ pint fish stock (see page 60)
salt and pepper
bouquet garni
20 pickling onions
12 button mushrooms
½ oz plain flour
chopped parsley (to garnish)
croûtes of fried bread (to garnish)

Method

Clean and prepare the fish, cutting it into neat pieces. Melt 1 oz of the butter in a sauté pan, add the onion and fish and cook gently until golden-brown. Flame with the red wine, allow to reduce by half, then add the stock. Season, add the bouquet garni and simmer very gently for about 20 minutes.

Blanch the pickling onions, drain and return to the pan with 1 oz butter and cook until golden-brown. Then add the mushrooms and continue cooking for 2-3 minutes. Remove the bouquet garni from the fish, add the onions and mushrooms and thicken the sauce with kneaded butter, made with remaining 1 oz butter and the flour ; continue cooking for 10 minutes.

Pile the fish in the centre of a hot serving dish, pour over the sauce, dust with chopped parsley and surround with the croûtes.

Matelote normande

good mixture of fish such as :
  1 lb rock salmon
  3 turbot steaks (each weighing 6
    oz)
  6 scallops
3 oz butter
½ pint white wine, or dry cider
salt and pepper
bouquet garni
20 pickling onions (partly
    cooked in a little butter)
½ oz plain flour
5-6 tablespoons double cream
heart-shaped croûtes of fried
    bread (to garnish)
chopped parsley (to garnish)

Method

Clean and prepare the fish, cutting it into neat pieces. Melt 2 oz butter in a sauté pan and when very hot, but not coloured, add the fish and cook for a few minutes on each side, but do not allow to colour. Moisten with the wine (or cider), season, and add bouquet garni and onions. Cover and cook over a very gentle heat for 20 minutes.

Then remove the fish and the onions and reduce the liquid in the pan by half. Knead the remaining butter with flour and add to the pan. When the sauce is thick and creamy, add the fresh cream and season well. Replace the fish and the onions and simmer together for 2-3 minutes. Dish up matelote, surround the fish with croûtes and dust with parsley.

Matelote de poisson

1 lb eels
2 turbot steaks
1 lb cod steak
1 wing of skate
½ pint white wine
¼ lb button mushrooms
nut of butter
squeeze of lemon juice

For court bouillon
2 medium-size carrots (sliced)
2 medium-size onions (sliced)
1 leek
bouquet garni (parsley root,
    bayleaf, thyme, celery, mace)
1½ pints water
salt and pepper

For sauce
1½ oz butter
1¼ oz plain flour
2 egg yolks
¼ pint cream

Method

Wash and clean all the fish and cut in thick slices or 'nuggets'.

Simmer together for 30 minutes all the ingredients for the court bouillon, seasoning with salt and pepper to taste ; then strain into a deep casserole. Place the fish in the casserole, eel first, then skate, turbot and, on the top, the nuggets of cod. Season, add the wine and simmer very gently for about 20 minutes.

Melt the butter for the sauce, blend in the flour and cook slowly until golden ; allow to cool. Then carefully tip on the liquid from the fish.

Bring to the boil and simmer for 10 minutes. Add the liaison of egg and cream, reheat carefully and spoon sauce over fish.

Garnish with the mushrooms, cooked in a nut of butter and a squeeze of lemon.

Calalou (Fish stew with okra)

1½ lb rock salmon
2 rashers of gammon bacon
2 oz salt belly pork
2 pints water
1 can (14 oz) okra
1 bayleaf
sprig of thyme, or 1 teaspoon of
    dried thyme
½ lb spinach (washed and cut in
    fine shreds)
2 tablespoons seasoned flour
1 oz butter
salt

Okra (sometimes called
'ladies' fingers') is native
to Africa : it was cooked in
Egypt over 2,000 years ago.
The plant, with its edible
5-sided pods, thrives only
in southern climates, but
fresh okra is occasionally
available in British markets.
If you buy it fresh, choose
clean-looking okra with
pods not more than 3 inches
long. The pods should snap
easily ; do not squeeze them
tightly and do not be dis-
mayed by a stringy liquid
which may cling to the knife
when cutting it.

Method

Cut the bacon and salt pork in
small cubes and cook gently to
draw out the fat, then tip this
off and keep on one side for
frying the fish. Cover the pork
and bacon with the water and
the juice from the can of okra,
add the bayleaf and thyme and
simmer gently until the pork is
soft. Add the spinach and okra
and cook for 5 minutes.

Meantime wash and dry the
fish, roll in seasoned flour and
fry in the reserved bacon fat until
brown. Add to the pan of stew
with the butter and a little salt if
necessary.

Watchpoint It is important
to taste the stew when the fish
is added before seasoning with
salt as it is quite possible that
the salt pork will have seasoned
it sufficiently.

Cover and cook very gently
until the fish is tender (about
5-10 minutes). Serve with a
dish of plainly boiled rice.

Fillets of sole mornay

2-2½ lb lemon, or Dover, sole (filleted)
salt
little onion (sliced)
6 peppercorns
½ bayleaf
6 tablespoons water
4 oz button mushrooms (optional)

For mornay sauce
1-1½ oz butter
¾ oz plain flour
½ pint milk
salt and pepper
1-2 rounded tablespoons grated
  cheese

Method

Wash, dry thoroughly and trim the fillets, removing both white and dark skin if this has not been done by the fishmonger. Fold the ends of each fillet under so that they appear the same size, and put in an ovenproof dish with a little salt, the onion, peppercorns, bayleaf and water. Cover with the washed sole bone, if available, to add extra flavour, cover with buttered paper and cook 10-12 minutes in the oven at 350°F or Mark 4.

To prepare mornay sauce: melt 1 oz of the butter in a pan, remove from heat and blend in the flour and milk. Season lightly, return pan to the heat and bring slowly to the boil, stirring continuously. Strain liquid from the fish, add it to the sauce and continue cooking for 2-3 minutes.

Meanwhile, wash the mushrooms quickly in salted water, trim stalks and slice. Cook quickly in the remaining butter for 1 minute. Arrange fish in a hot dish and spoon over the mushrooms.

Remove sauce from heat and beat in the cheese, a little at a time, reserving 1 dessertspoon. Cover fish with the sauce, sprinkle with reserved cheese and brown lightly under grill or in oven.

Sole bonne femme

4 double, or 8 single, fillets of
Dover, or lemon, sole
6 peppercorns
1 slice of onion
1 bayleaf
1 wineglass white wine
1 wineglass water
2 oz mushrooms (trimmed,
washed and sliced)
squeeze of lemon juice

For hollandaise sauce
1 onion (sliced)
2 tablespoons tarragon vinegar
1 egg yolk (beaten)
2 oz butter

For white wine sauce
1 oz butter
$\frac{1}{2}$ oz plain flour
$7\frac{1}{2}$ fl oz fish stock (using white
wine, see method)
5 tablespoons top of the milk
salt and pepper

Method

First prepare the hollandaise
sauce : add sliced onion to
vinegar and reduce to 1 teaspoon over gentle heat. Strain
on to the beaten yolk, standing
bowl in a bain-marie ; add $\frac{1}{4}$ oz
butter and beat until thick. Then
add the rest of the butter slowly,
beating well. When the consistency is of thick cream, cover
and set aside.

Set oven at 350°F or Mark 4.

To prepare the sole : skin,
wash and dry the fillets, fold in
half lengthways, put in a buttered
ovenproof dish, add peppercorns,
onion slice and bayleaf, pour
over the white wine and water.
Cover with buttered paper and
poach in pre-set oven for 15-20
minutes. Strain the liquid from
the fish and measure it —
there should be about $7\frac{1}{2}$ fl oz of
stock.

To make white wine sauce :
melt the butter in a saucepan,
add the flour — off the heat —
then pour on the fish stock. Stir
until thick, add milk and bring
quickly to the boil. Adjust
seasoning and simmer sauce
for 2-3 minutes to a coating
consistency.

Cook mushrooms quickly in
1 tablespoon of water and a
squeeze of lemon juice. Put
fillets on serving dish, coat with
the white wine sauce, scatter
on the mushrooms and then put
a tablespoon of the hollandaise
on each fillet. Glaze under the
grill and serve sole at once.

1 *Straining vinegar on to beaten egg yolk in the initial stages of hollandaise sauce*

2 *After butter is beaten into the egg yolk and vinegar the hollandaise sauce should have the consistency of thick cream*

3 *Pouring white wine over fillets of sole, which have been folded in half lengthways*

4 *Putting hollandaise sauce on sole and mushrooms after coating with white sauce*

Délices of sole Parmesan

1½-2 lb lemon, or Dover, sole
  (filleted)
1 tablespoon seasoned flour
1 egg (beaten)
4 tablespoons fresh breadcrumbs
2 tablespoons grated Parmesan
  cheese
3 oz butter (clarified)
2 small bananas
½ oz butter
juice of ¼ lemon
8 almonds (blanched and shredded)

Method

Cut the fillets of fish into thick finger-like strips and dry them well. Roll them in the seasoned flour, brush with egg and coat with the breadcrumbs and cheese mixed together, pressing them on to the fish with a palette knife. Then fry fillets in the clarified butter until crisp and golden-brown. Pile them into a hot serving dish (without draining) and keep warm.

Wipe out the frying pan with absorbent paper. Cut the bananas in thick slanting slices, drop the ½ oz butter in the pan and when foaming, add the bananas and fry quickly until brown. Pour over the lemon juice and add the almonds. Arrange the bananas and almonds around the fish and serve very hot.

Cutting the sole fillets into thick strips. The breadcrumbs and cheese mixture is used for coating the fish

The banana slices which accompany the sole are fried until brown in foaming butter

Délices of sole Parmesan with bananas and almonds

Sole Georgette

1 filleted sole (weighing 1½ lb)
4 large long-shaped potatoes
1 wineglass white wine
½ wineglass water
slice of onion
6 peppercorns
¾ oz butter
scant ¾ oz plain flour
salt and pepper
5 tablespoons top of milk
4 oz prawns (shelled)
grated cheese (to sprinkle)

Forcing bag and large rose pipe

Method

Set the oven at 375°F or Mark 5.

Scrub the potatoes well, dry and roll them in salt. Bake until tender (about 1½-2 hours).

Wash and dry the fillets; fold them over to the length of the potatoes. Place fillets in an ovenproof dish, pour over the wine and water, add the onion and peppercorns. Poach in a slow to moderate oven (325-350°F or Mark 3-4) for 10-12 minutes.

Melt the butter in a saucepan, stir in the flour and strain on the liquid from the fish. Season. Blend and stir until boiling. Add the top of the milk, adjust seasoning. Add 1-2 tablespoons of the sauce to the prawns to bind them.

When potatoes are soft, cut off the tops lengthways, scoop out the pulp, divide the prawn mixture evenly between the potatoes and place inside the skins. Lay a fillet of sole on top and coat with the rest of the sauce. Make a purée of the scooped-out potato and pipe round the edge of each potato skin; sprinkle with grated cheese and bake until brown in a quick oven (400°F or Mark 6). Alternatively, instead of making potato border, replace the 'lid' and reheat for a few minutes in the oven.

Serve each potato very hot in a napkin.

1 *Scooping out cooked potato from the skin to make container for fish; alongside are prawns mixed with a little of the sauce*
2 *Piping potato purée round edge of the potato skin after it has been filled*

1

2

Sole Georgette is browned quickly in the oven and served in a napkin

Sole meunière aux moules

6 fillets of sole, or 1 sole
(weighing 2 lb filleted)
1 quart mussels
bouquet garni
1 stick of celery
1 wineglass water
3-4 oz unsalted butter
seasoned flour
juice and grated rind of ½ lemon
1 tablespoon chopped parsley
pepper (ground from mill)
quarters of lemon (to garnish)

Method

Skin the fillets and, if using from whole sole, cut each one in half diagonally. Wash and dry them, and set aside.

Wash and scrape the mussels thoroughly and put into a roomy saucepan with the bouquet garni and stick of celery. Pour over a wineglass of water. Cover the pan and bring slowly to the boil, shaking occasionally. (The mussels will open as they cook.)

Take up the mussels, shell them and pull off the beards. Set the mussels aside in a little melted butter and keep warm.

Flour the fillets, heat a large thick frying pan and melt about 1 oz of the butter. When foaming, lay in the fillets, skinned side downwards. Cook fairly briskly for 3-4 minutes or until golden-brown and then turn over carefully and continue to fry on the other side.

Lift out the fillets on to a serving dish and overlap them down it (do not drain on paper). Put dish in the oven to keep warm.

To serve, wipe out the pan, reheat and drop in the remaining butter with the lemon rind. Cook until just turning colour, then add the lemon juice, mussels, parsley and pepper. Shake over the heat for a few seconds and then pour over the sole. Serve very hot with quarters of lemon, either arranged around the dish or handed separately.

1 *Arranging fillets of sole, which have been cooked in butter, down the dish*
2 *Pouring mussels, lemon, parsley and pepper mixture over fried soles*

Fillets of sole cooked in butter with mussels, lemon juice and parsley

Sole andalouse

2 soles (1½ lb each) — filleted
court bouillon (made with 1 bayleaf,
   1 slice of onion, 6 peppercorns,
   salt, ¼ pint water)
½ pint mayonnaise (made with 2 egg
   yolks, ½ pint olive oil, about 3 tea-
   spoons vinegar, or lemon juice,
   salt and pepper, pinch of dry
   mustard)
¼ clove of garlic (crushed with a
   little salt)
1 teaspoon tomato purée
½ teaspoon paprika pepper

For rice salad
5 oz long grain rice
½ cucumber
½ packet of frozen green peas, or
   cooked French beans, or ¼ lb each
   fresh peas and French beans
   (cooked)
4 oz carrot (diced and cooked)
4-5 tablespoons French dressing
salt and pepper

For garnish
1-2 caps of pimiento (shredded) and
   a little juice from the can
1 bunch of watercress

Method
Fold the fillets and lay them in a buttered ovenproof dish. Barely cover with all the ingredients for the court bouillon. Poach in a very moderate oven at 325-350°F or Mark 3-4 for about 12-15 minutes. Allow fish to cool.

Meanwhile cook the rice in plenty of salted, boiling water for 12 minutes or until tender. Drain and dry it thoroughly, then mix with the vegetables and French dressing ; season to taste.

Prepare the mayonnaise and thin it, if necessary, with 1 tablespoon of boiling water. Add crushed garlic, tomato purée and paprika pepper ; add a little juice from the canned pimiento to taste.

Arrange the rice salad down the centre of a serving dish. Place the fillets overlapping on the top and coat with the sauce. Garnish with pimiento and bouquets of watercress.

Sole éventail

2 soles (1¼ lb each) — filleted
  and skinned
juice of ½ lemon

For farce
12 oz-1 lb whiting (filleted) — to
  give approximately 8 oz
  minced fish
2 egg whites
¼ pint double cream
salt and pepper

For mayonnaise collée
½ pint mayonnaise
¼ oz (1 rounded teaspoon)
  gelatine
2½ fl oz aspic jelly

For garnish
8 button mushrooms (sliced and
  cooked)
1½-2 pints aspic jelly (see page 58)

This is a particularly good sole dish suitable for a buffet supper. The word 'éventail' means a fan in French and describes the way in which the finished fillets are arranged.

Method

Skin and trim the fillets, wash and dry them well, then bat them out carefully. Set oven at 325°F or Mark 3.

To prepare farce : gradually work minced fish with egg whites, then beat in the cream ; season and set aside.

Spread farce on the skinned side of each fillet ; fold over the tail section and smooth the sides. Make sure that each fillet is pointed at the end. Arrange fillets in a lightly buttered oven-proof dish, sprinkle with lemon juice, cover with a piece of foil or buttered paper and poach in pre-set very moderate oven for 12-15 minutes. Strain off liquor and leave the fillets to cool.

For the mayonnaise collée : dissolve gelatine in aspic jelly and stir into the mayonnaise. Wait until it is on the point of setting (as thick as cream) before coating the fillets.

Set fillets on a cake rack, with a large plate or tray underneath, and pour over the mayonnaise collée. Leave them for 10-12 minutes, then garnish with sliced mushrooms.

When set, baste fillets with a little cool aspic jelly.

Chop the remaining aspic, arrange it on a silver or stainless steel dish and place the fillets on top in the shape of a fan. Garnish with aspic croûtons (chopped into cubes).

Sole éventail — the stuffed fillets are arranged on aspic in the traditional fan shape

Fillets of sole in aspic

1 sole (filleted)
$\frac{1}{2}$ pint court bouillon
2 pints fish aspic
1 hard-boiled egg (sliced)
truffle, or pimiento
small cress, or watercress

For farce
1 oz butter
1 oz plain flour
$\frac{1}{4}$ pint milk
4 oz cooked shellfish (lobster, or
  scampi, or prawns) — chopped
salt and pepper
2-3 drops of lemon juice
1 egg yolk

4 dariole moulds

Method
First prepare the farce : melt
butter, stir in flour, add milk and
bring to the boil. Remove pan
from heat, add the chopped
shellfish, seasoning and lemon
juice. Add the egg yolk and cook
over gentle heat to bind (1-2
minutes). Leave farce to cool.

Prepare fillets, cutting them
in half if they are large ones.
Spread farce over each one, roll
them up neatly and tie loosely
with thread. Poach fillets in the
court bouillon in the oven at
350°F or Mark 4 for 10-12
minutes. Drain and leave them
to cool, then remove thread.

Line the moulds with aspic,
garnish with egg and truffle
or pimiento and set the decoration with a ayer of aspic. Put
in the fillets and fill up moulds
with aspic, adding it gradually
and allowing each portion to
set before adding more aspic.

Set a thin layer of aspic on an
oval silver dish. Unmould the
fillets and arrange in a slanting
line on the aspic. Garnish with
chopped aspic and cress.

Aspic jelly

$2\frac{1}{2}$ fl oz sherry
$2\frac{1}{2}$ fl oz white wine
2 oz gelatine
$1\frac{3}{4}$ pints cold stock
1 teaspoon white wine vinegar
2 egg whites

Method
Add wines to gelatine and set
aside. Pour cold stock into
scalded pan, add vinegar. Whisk
egg whites to a froth, add them
to the pan, set over moderate
heat and whisk backwards and
downwards - until the stock is
hot. Then add gelatine, which
by now will have absorbed the
wine, and continue whisking
steadily until boiling point has
been reached.

Stop whisking and allow liquid
to rise to the top of the pan ;
turn off heat or draw pan aside
and leave to settle for about 5
minutes, then bring it again to
the boil, draw pan aside once
more and leave liquid to settle.
At this point the liquid should
look clear ; if not, repeat the
boiling-up process.

Filter the jelly through a cloth
or jelly bag.

Sole Nantua

2 soles (1 lb each) — filleted
squeeze of lemon juice
2-3 tablespoons fish stock, or water

For farce
$\frac{3}{4}$ lb whiting
4 oz prawns (shelled — reserve
   shells for mayonnaise)
2 egg whites
$\frac{1}{4}$ pint double cream
salt and pepper

For mayonnaise collée
prawn shells
$\frac{1}{2}$ pint olive oil
$\frac{1}{2}$ teaspoon paprika pepper
2 egg yolks
squeeze of lemon juice
2$\frac{1}{2}$ fl oz aspic jelly (with 1 teaspoon
   gelatine dissolved in it)

For garnish
4 prawns
$\frac{1}{2}$ pint aspic jelly (for basting and
   chopping) — see page 58
1 bunch of watercress

Method

First prepare the farce : skin, wash and dry whiting, remove bones and mince or pound flesh and blend in with the prawns. Break egg whites lightly with a fork and gradually beat them into the fish mixture. Add the cream gradually and season. Set this farce aside. Set oven at 350°F or Mark 4.

Skin fillets of sole, wash and dry them, then bat out slightly and spread farce on to the skinned sides. Fold them over, lay in an ovenproof dish, squeeze over a little lemon juice and add fish stock (or water). Cover fish with a buttered paper and poach gently in pre-set moderate oven for 15 minutes. Strain liquid from fish and leave to cool.

To prepare mayonnaise : wash and dry prawn shells, pound them with oil and paprika ; leave for a little while and strain. Use this oil to make mayonnaise in usual way ; season and sharpen with lemon juice. Stir in aspic and gelatine.

Place fillets on a wire rack over a tray and coat with mayonnaise. When set, decorate each fillet with a prawn and baste with cool aspic ; leave to set thoroughly. Serve fillets on a bed of chopped aspic and garnish with bouquets of watercress.

Sole Nelson

2 Dover, or lemon, soles (each weighing 1¼ lb filleted)

For stock
sole bones
1 onion (sliced and blanched)
½ pint water
bouquet garni
6 peppercorns
salt
2-3 slices of lemon

For sauce
1 oz butter
scant 1 oz plain flour
¼ pint milk

For garnish
½ lb soft herring roes
2 tablespoons seasoned flour
2-3 tablespoons oil (for frying)
parisienne potatoes
1 tablespoon chopped parsley

Parisienne potatoes

Scoop out potato balls with a cutter, either plain boil them and toss in melted butter, or sauté them ; add chopped parsley.

Method

To prepare the fish stock : wash the fish bones well and put them in a pan with the onion, water, bouquet garni, seasoning and lemon slices and simmer gently for 15-20 minutes. Strain liquid and leave it to cool. Set oven at 350°F or Mark 4.

Place the fillets in an oven-proof dish, cover with the fish stock and cook in pre-set moderate oven for 8-10 minutes. Meanwhile roll the roes in the seasoned flour and fry them in the hot oil until golden-brown. Drain and keep hot.

To make the sauce : melt the butter, blend in the flour and cook for 2-3 seconds until straw coloured. Add ¼ pint of the liquor strained from the fish, stir until it thickens, then add the milk. Simmer for 3-5 minutes and test for seasoning. Dish up the fillets of fish, coat with the sauce and garnish with the fried roes and potatoes. Dust garnish well with the chopped parsley.

Sole en paupiettes

2 soles (each weighing 1¼-1½ lb filleted)
12 oz whiting, or fresh haddock, fillet (to give about 8 oz minced fish)
2 tablespoons hot milk
4 oz fresh white breadcrumbs
1½ oz butter
salt and pepper
2 egg yolks
8 frozen scampi (1 small packet)
few drops of lemon juice

For white wine sauce
2 wineglasses white wine
1 shallot (finely chopped)
1 oz butter
1 oz plain flour
8 fl oz fish stock (see page 60)
2 tablespoons double cream, or hollandaise sauce (see page 48)

For garnish
8 button mushrooms
½ oz butter
squeeze of lemon juice
fleurons of pastry (optional)

Method

Set the oven at 325°F or Mark 3.

Cut the sole fillets in half lengthways and bat out lightly. Mince the whiting (or haddock). Pour the hot milk over the breadcrumbs and leave them to soak for 5 minutes, then add the butter in small pieces. Pound the minced fish with the crumbs, season, and bind with the egg yolks.

Spread the fillets with this farce, put a scampi in the centre of each and roll up like a swiss roll. Set the paupiettes on their ends in a buttered ovenproof dish, sprinkle with a few drops of lemon juice and about 1-2 tablespoons of the fish stock, cover with a buttered paper and poach in pre-set very moderate oven for 15 minutes.

Meanwhile wash and trim the mushrooms and cook briskly with the butter and lemon juice.

To make the sauce : put the wine and shallot in a pan and boil until reduced to half quantity, then strain and set aside. Melt the butter, add the flour and cook gently for 2-3 seconds, until straw-coloured and marbled in appearance. Blend in the stock and wine, stir until boiling, then simmer gently for 3 minutes ; draw aside and beat in the cream (or hollandaise sauce).

Take up the fish, drain, arrange on a hot serving dish and place a mushroom on top of each. Spoon over the sauce and glaze under the grill. Garnish with fleurons if wished.

Sole Véronique

1½ lb sole (filleted)
1 wineglass water
½ wineglass white wine
6 peppercorns
1 slice of onion
4-6 oz green grapes
lemon juice

For sauce
1 oz butter
½ oz plain flour
salt and pepper
4 fl oz creamy milk, or single
  cream
1 egg yolk
parsley (chopped)

Method

Wash and dry fillets. Fold and place in a buttered ovenproof dish. Pour over the water and wine and add the peppercorns and onion. Cover with buttered paper and poach in the oven at 325-350°F or Mark 3-4 for 10-15 minutes.

Meanwhile peel and pip grapes. Sprinkle with lemon juice and keep covered until wanted.

To make sauce : melt butter in saucepan, stir in flour off heat, strain on the liquor from the fish. Blend and stir until boiling, season and draw aside. Mix cream and yolk together and add to the sauce. Thicken over the heat without boiling, then add grapes. Put sole on serving dish and spoon over the sauce. Sprinkle with chopped parsley.

Vinaigrette de sole aux ananas

2 soles (each weighing 1¼ lb
  filleted)
2½ fl oz water
juice of ½ lemon
slice of onion
salt
6 peppercorns
1 lb small new potatoes
5 tablespoons French dressing
1 fresh pineapple (peeled and cut
  in slices), or 4 slices of canned
  pineapple
little sugar
paprika pepper
½ lb tomatoes (skinned)
1 tablespoon chopped parsley

Method

Set oven at 350°F or Mark 4. Roll the fillets of sole and poach them in the water, with a little lemon juice, onion slice and seasoning, in pre-set oven for 10-12 minutes. When cooked, take out and leave to cool in the liquid.

Meanwhile cook the potatoes in their skins ; then peel, slice and sprinkle with French dressing while still hot. Season pineapple with a little lemon juice, sugar and paprika. Cut the tomatoes in four, remove the seeds and then cut flesh into strips. Arrange the potato salad down the centre of a serving dish, drain the sole and arrange on top. Surround with the pineapple slices. Mix the tomatoes with the remaining French dressing and parsley and spoon them over the fish.

Peeling cooked new potatoes to form base for vinaigrette de sole

Placing fillets on potatoes before arranging tomatoes on top

Vinaigrette de sole aux ananas, showing how the various ingredients are arranged for serving. This makes a most attractive party dish

Sole Joinville

4 slip soles (filleted, plus bones
  for stock)
$1\frac{1}{2}$ lb whiting, or hake, or 1 lb
  fresh haddock fillet
bouquet garni
1 carrot (sliced)
1 onion (sliced)
2 eggs (beaten)
5 tablespoons double cream
salt and pepper

For panade
$2\frac{1}{2}$ oz plain flour
2 oz butter
$\frac{3}{4}$ cup milk

For velouté sauce
1 oz butter
$\frac{1}{2}$ oz plain flour
$\frac{3}{4}$ cup fish stock (made from sole
  bones)
5 tablespoons single cream, or
  top of milk

For garnish
12 large prawns (unshelled)
$\frac{1}{2}$ lb button mushrooms
1 oz butter

For prawn butter
tail shells from prawns
1 oz unsalted butter

*7-inch diameter savarin, or ring,
mould*

François d'Orléans, **Prince
de Joinville** (who was the
third son of King Louis Phi-
lippe I) had many dishes
named after him, of which
this is the best known.

Method

Well grease the mould and set
oven at 325°F or Mark 3.

Trim the fillets of sole, remove
skin, wash and dry fillets
thoroughly and leave wrapped
in a cloth or absorbent paper
until wanted. Skin and bone the
whiting, hake or haddock and
pass twice through a mincer.
Check the weight of minced
fish — you must have at least
12 oz but not more than 1 lb.

Make the stock by putting
fish bones into a pan, adding
water to cover and bouquet
garni, sliced carrot and onion.
Bring to boil and simmer gently
for about 30 minutes, then strain
and set aside.

To prepare the panade : sift
$2\frac{1}{2}$oz flour on to a piece of paper
and set aside. Cut the 2 oz
butter in pieces, put in a pan,
add milk and bring slowly to

*Lining the mould with sole fillets
needs some skill. Place them, skinned side up, overlapping slightly
with no gaps in between*

the boil. Draw the pan off the heat and at once tip in all the sifted flour. Heat until smooth, turn on to a plate and leave to cool. Work the panade, beaten eggs and minced fish together and when thoroughly mixed and quite smooth, stir in the double cream and season well.

Line the savarin, or ring, mould with the fillets of sole, skinned side uppermost, overlapping slightly so that there are no gaps. Fill this lined mould with the fish panade and fold the ends of the fillets over the top. Cover with a piece of thickly-buttered greaseproof paper and cook au bain-marie in the pre-set oven for 40-45 minutes or until the fillets of sole are firm to the touch.

Meanwhile prepare garnish and prawn butter: peel away the tail shells only of the prawns; put the prawns between two buttered plates and set aside for heating. Trim and wash the mushrooms and put in a small pan with $\frac{1}{2}$ oz butter and seasoning.

Pound the prawn tail shells with 1 oz butter until smooth. This is best done with a pestle and mortar, but failing this, use the end of a rolling pin in a small basin. Rub this prawn butter through a strainer and set aside.

Now make velouté sauce: melt the butter in a pan, add the flour, cook gently to a pale straw colour, draw pan aside and blend in the stock. Return pan to the heat, stir until the sauce begins to thicken, then add the cream and bring to the boil. Cook for 2-3 minutes, draw aside and beat in the prawn butter, a small piece at a time. Taste and adjust the seasoning.

Put the prawns into the oven for 5 minutes to heat through; sauté the mushrooms quickly for 1 minute.

Turn the mould on to a hot serving dish and leave for 2-3 minutes. Then lift mould carefully and wipe up any juice that may come away from the fish with a clean cloth or absorbent paper. Then coat with the velouté sauce before filling the centre with the mushrooms; garnish with prawns.

This dish doesn't really need any accompanying vegetables, particularly when it is preceded by soup. But if you feel that a main course is incomplete without vegetables, serve 'fish' potatoes and French beans.

After cooking the fish panade wrapped in fillets, turn out mould and coat with sauce

Sole Joinville continued

When the mould has been turned out and coated with the velouté sauce, the centre is filled with sauté mushrooms and garnished with large prawns in their shells. Serve this mould on its own or with 'fish' potatoes and French beans

Sole mâconnaise

2 Dover, or lemon, soles (each
  weighing 1¼ lb filleted)
1 wineglass red Mâcon
½ wineglass water
6 peppercorns
bayleaf
slice of onion
salt
½ lb small pickling onions
¾ oz butter
1 teaspoon caster sugar
¼ lb mushrooms
squeeze of lemon juice

For sauce
1 oz butter
¾ oz plain flour
2½ fl oz top of milk, or single
  cream

Method

Set oven at 350°F or Mark 4.

Trim and skin the fish, then
wash and dry it. Fold the fillets
over and lay them in a buttered
ovenproof dish. Pour over the
wine and water, then add the
peppercorns, bayleaf, onion
slice and a pinch of salt. Cover
with a buttered paper and poach
in pre-set moderate oven for
8-10 minutes.

Meanwhile blanch the pickling onions for about 5 minutes,
drain and return them to the
pan with ½ oz butter, a pinch of
salt and the sugar. Cover and
cook gently until the onions are
tender and light brown.

Peel and trim the mushrooms
and cook quickly in 1 tablespoon water, ¼ oz butter and a
squeeze of lemon for 1-2
minutes. Keep both the mushrooms and onions hot.

Meanwhile prepare the
sauce : melt the butter in the
pan, blend in the flour and
cook for 2-3 minutes until
marbled. Strain on the liquor
from the fish, stir until boiling,
add top of milk (or single cream)
and simmer for 2-3 minutes.
Test for seasoning.

Place the fish on a hot serving
dish, spoon over the sauce and
surround with the onions and
mushrooms.

Sole Lasserre

1½-2 lb sole (filleted)
1 shallot (finely chopped)
2 oz flat mushrooms (sliced)
salt
6 peppercorns
1 wineglass white wine, or water
and a squeeze of lemon juice
4 oz button mushrooms
1 oz butter
béchamel sauce (made with 1 oz
butter, 1 oz flour, ½ pint
flavoured milk)
8-10 asparagus spears (cooked)
1 egg yolk
1 oz extra butter

For rich shortcrust pastry
6 oz plain flour
3 oz butter
1 oz shortening
1 egg yolk
1-2 tablespoons water

8-inch diameter flan ring

Method

Make up the rich shortcrust pastry and chill. Then line flan ring with it and bake blind.

Cut each fillet into two or three pieces and put in a buttered ovenproof dish with the shallot and flat mushrooms. Season with salt, set the peppercorns to one side, and pour over the wine (or water and lemon juice). Cover with buttered paper and poach in pre-set moderate oven (350°F or Mark 4) for 10-15 minutes.

Meanwhile chop the button mushrooms, soften them in the butter and place at the bottom of the warm pastry case. Prepare béchamel sauce. Pour liquid from the fish into a saucepan, reduce to about half and add it to the béchamel sauce. Place the fish and asparagus in the pastry case on top of the mushrooms. Beat egg yolk and extra butter (a small piece at a time) into the sauce and adjust seasoning ; spoon over fish.

Asparagus is an extra luxury with this delicious fish flan

Sole portugaise

2 soles (each weighing 1½ lb
   filleted) — with bones
bouquet garni
slice of onion
clove of garlic
squeeze of lemon juice
2½ fl oz water
2 tablespoons double cream

For soubise purée
4 medium-size onions (finely
   sliced)
¼ pint milk
1 oz butter
½ oz plain flour
salt and pepper

For tomato sauce
1 lb tomatoes
1 dessertspoon tomato purée
1 tablespoon water
salt and pepper
1½ oz butter
½ oz plain flour
¼ pint creamy milk

For garnish
4 large tomatoes (skinned)
½ oz butter

Method

First prepare the soubise purée :
blanch the onions and strain,
return to the pan with the milk
and cook slowly until soft.
Strain again. Reserve the milk
and rub the onions through a
fine strainer. Melt the butter,
blend in the flour and the onion
milk, season and stir until
boiling ; add this to the onion
purée. Return mixture to the
pan and simmer until it is the
consistency of thick cream.
Test for seasoning, cover and
keep warm.

To prepare the tomato sauce :
wipe the tomatoes, cut them in
four, squeeze away the seeds
and cut flesh roughly. Put in a
pan with the tomato purée,
water, salt and pepper ; cook
slowly for 10 minutes, stirring
occasionally, and then strain.
Melt the butter in another pan,
add the flour and blend in the
milk. Stir over gentle heat until
it comes to the boil, then add
the strained tomato pulp. Simmer for 5 minutes, cover and
keep on one side. Set oven at
350°F or Mark 4.

Wash and dry the fillets of
fish and place in a buttered
ovenproof dish with the
bouquet garni, onion, and garlic.
Pour over the lemon juice and
water, cover with the bones of
the fish and poach in pre-set
moderate oven for 8-10 minutes.

Cut the 4 tomatoes in half
across, and scoop out the
centre with the point of a
teaspoon. Season, and pour a
small quantity of melted butter
into each tomato cup. Cook in
the oven for about 5 minutes.
Put the soubise purée in a
serving dish and arrange the
tomatoes on top. Place a fillet
of sole on top of each tomato,
strain the fish liquor into the
tomato sauce, bring to the boil
and add the cream. Test for
seasoning and coat the whole
dish with the sauce.

Sole Suchet

2 soles (1¼ lb each) — filleted
1 wineglass white wine
1-2 drops of lemon juice
2 medium-size carrots
¼ oz butter
1 glass Madeira, or medium
   sherry
4-8 button mushrooms (sautéd)
   — optional
½ pint béchamel sauce
2 tablespoons double cream
3 medium-size tomatoes

For farce
10 oz whiting (filleted) — to give
   about 6 oz minced fish
1 egg white (lightly broken)
4 fl oz double cream
salt and pepper

Method

First prepare farce : wash and dry whiting, remove skin and any bones, then mince flesh. Work this with the egg white added gradually, then beat in the cream. Season to taste.

Skin the fillets, wash and dry them well, then bat out. Thickly spread skinned side of fillets with the farce, fold them over, neaten the sides and lay them in a lightly buttered oven-proof dish. Pour over white wine and lemon juice and cover with a buttered paper. Set oven at 325°F or Mark 3.

Cut the red part of the carrots into fine strips, discarding the hard woody core, put them into a small pan with butter and sherry. Cover pan tightly and simmer for 6-7 minutes until carrot is tender.

Poach fish in pre-set oven for 12-15 minutes, strain fish liquor into béchamel sauce, simmer until it is of a creamy consistency, add the cream, then the carrots. Scald and skin tomatoes, cut them in half, then grill lightly or bake them in the oven for 10 minutes.

Arrange fillets of sole in a hot serving dish, coat with the sauce and garnish each fillet with a tomato half and a button mushroom.

Sole Gustave

2 soles (1¼ lb each) — filleted
1 wineglass white wine
½ wineglass water
1 shallot (sliced)
6 peppercorns
3 oz button mushrooms
½ oz butter
squeeze of lemon juice
6-8 asparagus spears
    (cooked)
2-3 tomatoes (according to size)
    — skinned, quartered, seeds
    removed and shredded
fleurons of puff pastry

For hollandaise sauce
3 tablespoons white wine
    vinegar
2 egg yolks (beaten)
3 oz butter (unsalted)

For white wine sauce
7½ fl oz fish liquor
¾ oz butter
scant ¾ oz plain flour
good 2½ fl oz milk
2-3 tablespoons double cream
salt and pepper

This dish was named after the chef of a little French restaurant which flourished in London in the twenties.

Method

Trim the asparagus and tie in a bundle with fine string. Have ready a deep pan of boiling salted water and stand the asparagus spears in this, stalk end down ; cook gently, covered, for 12-15 minutes or until green part is tender. Drain and set aside.

Watchpoint The green tips should stand above the water and cook just in the steam.

Skin, wash and dry the fillets, fold them, then place in a buttered ovenproof dish and pour over the wine and water ; add the shallot and peppercorns at the side of the dish. Cover with buttered paper and poach in the oven at 350°F or Mark 4 for 12 minutes.

Meanwhile prepare hollandaise sauce (see method, page 48).

Strain liquor from fish, and reserve 7½ fl oz.

To make wine sauce : melt the butter, stir in flour and blend in reserved fish liquor. Bring it to boil, then add milk and cream. Boil it again for 2-3 minutes, season and draw pan aside. Cool this sauce slightly and beat in hollandaise sauce ; keep it warm.

Slice mushrooms, sauté in butter and squeeze of lemon juice. Dish up fish, arrange mushrooms, asparagus and tomatoes on top. Spoon over the sauce and glaze fish under the grill. Garnish the dish with the fleurons of pastry.

Sole Colbert

4 slip soles (8-12 oz each) —
  skinned
seasoned flour
beaten egg
dried white breadcrumbs (for
  coating)
quarters of lemon (for serving)
2 oz maître d'hôtel butter

Deep fat bath

This dish and others are
named after **Jean-Baptiste
Colbert,** a statesman and
patron of the arts in the
reign of Louis XIV.

Method
With a small sharp knife make
a cut right down the centre
along the backbone, on what
was the white-skinned side
of the sole (the side with the
thinner fillets). With short,
sharp strokes, lift the fillets up
from this side, down to the fin
bones (but keep attached).
Leave on the heads, trim the
sides with the scissors and
square the tails. Wash and dry
thoroughly. Roll in a little
seasoned flour, not forgetting
the insides of the raised fillets.
Brush with beaten egg and roll
in crumbs, pressing them on
firmly.

Have ready a deep fat bath,
one-third filled with hot oil or
fat. Gently slide in the fish, one
or two at a time, depending on
the size of the bath, and fry
for 5-6 minutes until golden-
brown. Drain well.

With the scissors snip back
bone at head and tail, then
gently pull it out. Dish up fish
on a hot serving dish and put a
strip of butter down the centre
of each in place of the backbone. Reheat in the oven for
1-2 minutes (350°F or Mark 4)
before serving with quarters of
lemon.

Maître d'hôtel butter

2 oz unsalted butter
1 dessertspoon chopped parsley
few drops of lemon juice
salt and pepper

Method
Soften the butter on a plate
with a palette knife, then add
parsley, lemon juice and seasoning to taste.

Serve chilled, in pats.

Sole in white wine

2 soles (1¼ lb each) — filleted
1 lemon
salt and pepper

For white wine sauce
1 wineglass white wine
1 shallot (finely chopped)
6 peppercorns
1 blade of mace
1 egg yolk (beaten)
3½ oz butter
1 oz plain flour
½ pint fish stock

For garnish
4-6 mushrooms
¼ oz butter

Method

Skin the fillets, wash and dry them well, then fold and place in a buttered ovenproof dish, adding a squeeze of lemon juice ; season and cover with a buttered paper. Set fish on one side. Set oven at 325°F or Mark 3.

Meanwhile prepare first part of the white wine sauce ; put the wine, shallot and seasonings in a pan and reduce to 1 teaspoon. Strain on beaten egg yolk, stand bowl in a bain-marie, add ¼ oz butter and beat until thick. Then add 2 oz butter, a ¼ oz at a time, beating well. When sauce is the consistency of whipped cream, cover pan and set aside.

Place fillets of sole in pre-set very moderate oven and poach for about 10 minutes.

Wash and trim mushrooms, slice or quarter them, depending on their size, and sauté in ¼ oz butter, adding seasoning and a squeeze of lemon juice.

Now continue with the sauce : melt remaining 1¼ oz butter, add the flour and cook roux slowly until it is a pale straw colour, for 5 seconds. Remove pan from heat, add the fish stock and blend until sauce is smooth. Season, return pan to heat, stir until sauce is boiling, then leave to simmer for 5 minutes.

Arrange fillets in a warm serving dish, scatter over the mushrooms. Beat the butter sauce into the velouté one and spoon it over the fish. Glaze under the grill before serving.

Stuffed sole with prawns and mushrooms

4-5 slip soles (8-12 oz each)
2 oz butter (melted)
2 tablespoons fresh white
  breadcrumbs
1 bunch of watercress (to
  garnish)

For filling
3 oz button mushrooms (sliced)
1 oz butter
$\frac{1}{2}$ oz plain flour
good $\frac{1}{4}$ pint milk
salt and pepper
3 oz prawns (shelled)
1 tablespoon double cream

Method
Have the sole skinned on both sides but with the heads left on. With a sharp knife make a cut right down the centre along the backbone, then raise the fillets on each side of it down to the fins, but leave attached. Turn the fish over and repeat the process.

With the scissors, snip through the backbone at head and tail and remove it ; trim away outside fringe of fins.

Well brush a baking sheet with melted butter and lay the soles on this. Set aside.

To prepare the filling : sauté mushrooms in a pan in half the butter for 2-3 minutes. Draw aside, add remaining butter and stir in the flour. Blend in the milk and stir until boiling. Draw aside, season lightly, and add prawns and cream. Put this filling into the soles, reshape and brush with melted butter. Sprinkle with crumbs, pressing them on well. Pour over melted butter and bake in oven at 375°F or Mark 5 for about 15 minutes. Finish under the grill, if necessary, to make sure the crumbs are golden in colour. Lift off soles carefully with a fish slice on to a hot serving dish and garnish with the watercress.

Souchet of sole (Fish with consommé)

4 slip soles (each fish weighing
    about $\frac{1}{2}$ lb filleted)
little lemon juice
salt and pepper
few drops of Tabasco sauce

For consommé
3 pints good strong veal, or
    chicken, stock (well flavoured
    with vegetables and seasoned)
$\frac{1}{4}$ pint white wine
$2\frac{1}{2}$ fl oz sherry
3 egg whites

For garnish
3 carrots
1 head of celery
2 leeks
nut of butter

If slip soles are not available, use fillets of small lemon, or witch, soles. This quantity serves 8 as a first course.

Method

First clarify the stock : turn it into a large scalded saucepan, then add the wine, sherry, and egg whites whipped to a froth.

Whisk backwards over moderate heat until at boiling point, then stop whisking and allow the mixture to come to the top of the pan undisturbed. Draw pan aside. Repeat this once more, again without disturbing the liquid ; draw aside and leave to settle. Then pour through a scalded cloth.

Skin the fillets, roll them up neatly and put into an ovenproof dish with a little water, lemon juice and salt to flavour. Cook in the oven (at 325°F or Mark 3) for 10 minutes. If preferred, they may be steamed between two plates with just a little seasoning and a squeeze of lemon ; this will take about 12-15 minutes.

Meanwhile prepare the garnish. Slice the red part only of the carrot into thin julienne strips. Treat the celery and the green part of the leeks in the same way. Put the garnish into boiling salted water and simmer for one minute. Then drain, refresh and return to the pan with a good nut of butter. Cover slowly and cook gently until tender (3-4 minutes).

When ready to serve, put 2 fillets in each soup plate or bowl. Reheat the consommé, add the garnish, seasoning and Tabasco to it, then carefully pour a ladleful of the soup over each serving of fish. Serve hot with thin brown bread and butter.

Mousseline of sole

4 slip soles (filleted)
6 oz frozen prawns (thawed
  overnight in refrigerator)
about ¾ pint aspic (see page 58)
½ pint mayonnaise (made with
  the yolks of 4 eggs)
watercress (to garnish) — optional

For mousseline
1½ lb hake, or fresh haddock
whites of 4 eggs
½ pint double cream
salt and pepper

Ring mould (1¼-1½ pints capacity)

This quantity serves 6-8 people as a first course.

Method

Skin the fillets and bat them out slightly to flatten. Well butter the ring mould. Arrange the fillets in this, skin side uppermost. See that the fillets overlap slightly, so that the bottom and sides of the mould are completely covered, and set aside.

To make mousseline : skin the hake (or haddock), mince it finely, then put into a bowl. Break the egg whites with a fork, then add them to fish, a little at a time, beating well between each addition. (If preferred, fish and egg white could be worked in a blender.) Then pass mixture through a wire sieve, return to the bowl and add the cream a little at a time. Season well. Fill the mould with the mousseline, making sure it comes level with the top. Reserve any that is left over. Fold the tips of the fillets over on to the mousseline. Cover with a piece of buttered foil, or paper, and steam gently, or poach in a bain-marie, in the oven (set at 350°F or Mark 4), for about 45 minutes.

Then allow to cool. Before the mousseline is completely cold, turn it on to a serving dish. With absorbent paper, wipe round the dish well to remove any liquid and set aside. Meanwhile poach the remaining mousseline to form quenelles, shaping them with two tablespoons ; drain well. Add prawns to the quenelles. Cool the aspic to setting point, then spoon it over the sole. Baste well and leave to set.

Clean round the dish again and put 1 tablespoon of the mayonnaise in the centre. Put in the quenelles and prawns, piling them up well, then coat with the remaining mayonnaise or, if preferred, thin the mayonnaise a little and pour it round, serving the rest separately. Garnish, if wished, with a little watercress.

Sole Walewska

2 Dover soles ($1\frac{1}{4}$-$1\frac{1}{2}$ lb each)
  — filleted
8 slices of lobster meat, or
  scampi (canned)
8 slices of truffle (optional)
$2\frac{1}{2}$ fl oz fish stock (made from
  the bones and trimmings)
  — see page 60

For sauce
1 oz butter
$\frac{3}{4}$ oz plain flour
$\frac{1}{4}$ pint fish stock
$2\frac{1}{2}$ fl oz double cream
1 oz grated Parmesan cheese

This is a classic dish and is sometimes made with a lobster butter sauce in place of a velouté one. 'A la Walewska' denotes a method of preparing fish, especially fillets of sole, with lobster and truffle garnish and mornay sauce.

Method
Skin fillets, wash and dry them, then bat them out. Set oven at 325°F or Mark 3.

Place a piece of lobster (or scampi) meat and a slice of truffle on each fillet. Fold them over and arrange in a buttered ovenproof dish ; pour over $2\frac{1}{2}$ fl oz fish stock. Poach fish in preset very moderate oven for 10-12 minutes.

To prepare sauce : melt the butter, add flour and cook roux for 1-2 seconds ; pour on fish stock, stir and bring to boil. Simmer sauce for 3-4 minutes, draw pan aside, add cream, $\frac{3}{4}$ oz cheese, and stir gently.

Dish up fish, spoon over sauce, sprinkle with rest of cheese and glaze under grill.

Sole à l'indienne

2 filleted soles (each weighing $1\frac{1}{4}$ lb)
salt
6 peppercorns
juice of $\frac{1}{2}$ lemon
1 lemon (to garnish)
paprika pepper (to garnish)

For curry cream sauce
1 tablespoon chopped onion
2 tablespoons oil
1 clove of garlic (chopped)
1 dessertspoon curry powder
$\frac{1}{2}$ pint tomato juice
salt and pepper
2-3 slices of lemon
1 tablespoon apricot jam
$\frac{1}{2}$ pint mayonnaise

For rice mixture
4 oz long grain rice
4 oz firm button mushrooms
squeeze of lemon juice
salt and pepper
4 oz prawns (shelled)
4 tablespoons French dressing

Method

Trim, wash and dry the fillets. Fold them and place in a buttered ovenproof dish ; season with salt, lay the peppercorns on one side and squeeze lemon juice over the fillets. Cover with a buttered paper and poach in a very moderate oven, pre-set at 350°F or Mark 4, for 8-10 minutes. Cool and drain.

To make curry cream sauce : soften the onion in the oil with the chopped garlic. Add the curry powder and cook for a few minutes, then add the tomato juice. Simmer for 7-10 minutes, then add seasoning and the lemon slices. Stir in the jam and strain the liquid ; cool it slightly, add the mayonnaise and adjust seasoning.

Cook the rice in boiling salted water for about 12 minutes ; drain, refresh and dry it. Trim the mushrooms, wash them quickly in salted water, then slice them and cook quickly for 1 minute with a squeeze of lemon and salt and pepper to taste ; allow to cool. Mix the rice, prawns and mushrooms together ; moisten with the French dressing and spoon on to the serving dish.

Arrange the fillets of fish on the rice and coat them with the sauce. Garnish each fillet with a thin slice of lemon dusted with paprika. Serve remaining sauce separately.

Sole parisienne

2 soles (each weighing 1¼ lb
  filleted)
¼ pint water
½ lemon
1-2 oz sliced cooked button
  mushrooms
about ¾ pint liquid aspic (to baste)
  —see page 58
1 pint aspic jelly (chopped)

For fish and mushroom
  mousseline
4 oz button mushrooms
12 oz whiting (filleted and finely
  chopped to give 6 oz minced)
½ oz butter
1 egg white
3-4 fl oz double cream
salt and pepper

For mayonnaise collée
½ pint mayonnaise
2½ fl oz liquid aspic
1 teaspoon gelatine

Method

Set oven at 350°F or Mark 4.
Trim the sole fillets, wash and
dry, and bat out or flatten each
with the blade of a heavy knife
or cutlet bat.

To prepare mousseline : chop
mushrooms finely and cook in
the ½ oz butter for 3-4 minutes
until dry. Turn out to cool. Skin
and mince the whiting, put it
into a basin and work in the egg
white (lightly broken with a
fork) by degrees. Add the
mushrooms. Beat in the cream
gradually and season.

Spread the fillets on the skin
side with the mousseline farce.
Draw the tail section over and
smooth the sides. Lay the
fillets in a lightly buttered ovenproof dish, pour on the water
and squeeze over the lemon.
Season and cover with buttered
paper and poach in the pre-set
moderate oven for 10-15
minutes. When cooked, take
out of oven and leave the fish
to cool in the liquid.

Dissolve the gelatine in the
2½ fl oz liquid aspic over gentle
heat and add this to the
mayonnaise. Place the fillets on
a cake rack and, when absolutely cold, coat with mayonnaise, which should be thick
and on the point of setting.
Have ready the mushroom
slices and arrange them on top
of each fillet. Leave for 15
minutes. Baste with cool aspic
and leave to set. To dish up, set
the fillets on chopped aspic.

Oily fish

Stewed eels and poached salmon may sound poles apart, but in fact they are very similar types of fish. Both are of the type known as oily fish, which means that the oil is distributed throughout the flesh rather than collected in the liver. This makes for a richer and coarser textured fish than the white fish.

Cooking oily fish is a less refined affair than for white fish — the grilled fish with a touch of savoury butter alone will provide the tastiest possible meal in a hurry. Imagine, then, what can be produced if you are prepared to go just a little further and make something more elaborate. Salmon Koulibiac is a classic Russian pastry dish to delight your friends. Stuffed trout or herrings in white wine will make your table equally renowned.

For something just a little unusual without being extravagant try the pâté bretonne on page 82. This makes a change from the delicious but ubiquitous liver pâtés and is simple and inexpensive to make.

When shopping for fish, don't forget to tell the fishmonger whether you want the heads left on or taken off. And if you are cleaning and filleting your own, once again you can follow our instructions on page 150.

Eels en matelote

2 lb eels
1½ oz butter
1 onion (finely chopped)
2 wineglasses red wine
½ pint fish stock — see page 60
salt and pepper
bouquet garni
12 pickling onions
12 button mushrooms
kneaded butter
chopped parsley (to garnish)
croûtons (to garnish)

Method
Wash eels thoroughly, dry well and cut into 3-inch lengths (if this has not been done by fishmonger). Melt 1 oz butter in a shallow stewpan, add finely chopped onion and prepared eel; cook gently until golden-brown. Flame with red wine, reduce by half, and then add stock. Season, add bouquet garni and simmer very gently for about 20 minutes.

Blanch pickling onions, drain and return to pan with remaining ½ oz butter; cook until golden-brown. Then add mushrooms and continue cooking for 2-3 minutes. Remove bouquet garni from eels, add onions and mushrooms and thicken sauce with kneaded butter; continue cooking for 10 minutes. Pile fish in centre of a hot serving dish, pour over sauce, dust with chopped parsley and surround with croûtons.

Pâté bretonne

3 herrings (filleted and skinned)
1-2 tablespoons lemon juice
1 tablespoon finely chopped herbs
¼ teaspoon ground nutmeg
¼ teaspoon ground allspice
salt and pepper
clarified butter (for serving)

For farce
2 herrings (filleted and skinned)
3 hard-boiled eggs
4 oz rice (cooked till tender in veal, or chicken, stock)
1 large mushroom (chopped)
1 egg (beaten)

Method
Set oven at 350°F or Mark 4.

Marinate the 3 filleted herrings in the lemon juice, herbs, spices and seasoning while preparing the farce.

Pound the 2 herrings with the yolks of the hard-boiled eggs, mix in the cooked rice and chopped mushroom and pass this mixture through a fine sieve or Mouli. Season and bind with the beaten egg. Place half the mixture in a buttered terrine and arrange the marinated fillets on top, then cover with the remaining farce. Stand the dish in a bain-marie and cook in pre-set oven for 45-50 minutes.

Leave to get cold and pour over a little clarified butter before serving. Hand hot toast and butter separately.

Herrings in white wine

2 herring fillets in wine (these can be bought in most delicatessens)
lemon juice, or wine vinegar
salt and pepper
2 tablespoons long grain rice
2-3 tablespoons oil
1 tablespoon wine vinegar
1 teaspoon made English mustard
2 medium-size dessert apples (Cox or Pippin)
lettuce leaves

Method

Cut the herring fillets in diagonal strips, sprinkle them well with lemon juice (or vinegar) and season. Leave for at least 1 hour. Boil the rice in plenty of salted water, drain and dry.

When ready to serve, mix the oil and vinegar together, season well, add the mustard and mix this dressing with the herrings. Peel and slice apples and add to the herrings with the rice. Serve in a bowl or on lettuce leaves on individual plates.

Serve herrings in white wine as a tasty starter

Salmon steaks en chaudfroid

12 salmon steaks (about 8 oz
  each)
2 pints court bouillon
1 tablespoon olive oil
1 shallot (finely chopped)
1 dessertspoon paprika pepper
1 dessertspoon tomato purée
juice strained from seeds of the
  tomato garnish
$1\frac{1}{2}$ pints mayonnaise
$\frac{3}{4}$ oz gelatine
$\frac{3}{4}$ pint aspic jelly (see page 58)

To garnish
$1\frac{1}{2}$ pints aspic jelly
few sprigs of chervil, or strips
  of cucumber skin
12 tomatoes (skinned, seeds
  removed, and chopped)
$\frac{1}{2}$ lb shelled prawns, or shrimps

This quantity serves 8 people.

Method
Set oven at 350°F or Mark 4.

Cover the fish with hot court bouillon and poach the fish steaks in pre-set oven for about 20 minutes. Allow to cool a little in the liquid, then remove the skin and bones. Divide each steak in two and bind in muslin, then press between two plates until cold.

Meanwhile heat the oil, add the shallot and cook for a few minutes to soften it. Then add the paprika, tomato purée and strained juice from the tomato seeds and cook for 2-3 minutes ; strain and cool. Place the fish steaks on a cake rack with a tray underneath.

Flavour the mayonnaise with tomato and paprika mixture ; dissolve the gelatine in the $\frac{3}{4}$ pint of aspic over gentle heat and add to the mayonnaise. When on the point of setting, baste over the salmon steaks.

Decorate each steak with the chervil or strips of cucumber skin (dipped in aspic) and then baste again with cool aspic. Arrange on a serving platter and garnish with a salpicon of the tomatoes, prawns and remaining aspic jelly (chopped).

After being poached the salmon steaks are divided in two and the skin and bones are removed

Coating salmon steaks with the flavoured mayonnaise and aspic mixture on the point of setting

Salmon mousse Nantua

8 oz cooked salmon (free from skin and bone)
$\frac{1}{2}$ pint cold béchamel sauce
$\frac{1}{4}$ pint mayonnaise
salt and pepper
scant $\frac{1}{2}$ oz gelatine (dissolved in 2-3 tablespoons light stock, or water)
1 small carton ($2\frac{1}{2}$ fl oz) double cream (lightly whipped)
2 oz prawns, or shrimps (coarsely chopped)

To finish
2 fl oz thick mayonnaise
tomato juice
Tabasco sauce
1 egg (hard-boiled)
watercress
extra prawns (optional)

6-7 inch diameter top (No. 1 or 2 size) soufflé dish, or cake tin

Method

Lightly oil the dish or tin. Pound or work the salmon until smooth. Add the béchamel sauce and mayonnaise to salmon, a little at a time. Season, fold in the dissolved gelatine, cream and prawns.

Turn mousse at once into the prepared mould and leave to set. Turn out, coat with mayonnaise, lightened with a little tomato juice and seasoned with Tabasco sauce.

To garnish : sieve the yolk and shred the white of the hard-boiled egg and sieve over the mousse ; arrange sprigs of watercress and extra prawns round it.

Salmon flan Valençay

2 salmon steaks (each weighing 12 oz)
1 wineglass white wine
12 oz quantity of puff pastry
4 oz shelled prawns (chopped)
4 oz mushrooms (chopped)
salt and pepper
$2\frac{1}{2}$ fl oz double cream
1 egg (beaten)
$1\frac{1}{2}$ oz maître d'hôtel butter (see page 73)

8-inch diameter flan ring

This flan was probably named after the château Valençay, at one time owned by Talleyrand, the French statesman and gastronome.

Method

Skin, bone and slice salmon steaks, divide each slice into two and marinate them in the wine for about 2 hours.

Set oven at 425°F or Mark 7. Roll out just over half of the pastry and line the flan ring with it. Lay salmon slices in flan, scatter over the prawns, mushrooms and seasoning. Pour over the cream.

Roll out remaining pastry and cover the flan ; trim the edges and decorate top with pastry leaves, if wished. Brush over a little beaten egg and bake in pre-set hot oven for 45-50 minutes.

Just before serving, remove flan ring and slit top edge of pastry enough to slip in savoury butter. Serve at once.

Quenelles Nantua

For salmon mousseline
1 ¼ lb salmon (to give approximately
  ¾ lb when skinned, boned
  and minced)
3 egg whites (lightly broken)
7½ fl oz double cream
salt and pepper

For prawn butter
½ pint prawns
1-2 oz butter

For bouchées
6 oz quantity of puff pastry
8 oz salmon steak
1 wineglass water
squeeze of lemon juice
4 oz button mushrooms (sliced)
½ oz butter

For Nantua sauce
½ pint strong fish stock (made
  from sole bones) — see page 60
1 oz butter
¾ oz plain flour
1 wineglass double cream, or
  creamy milk

*2½ inch diameter fluted cutter, 1½ inch
diameter cutter (fluted or plain)*

Method

First prepare salmon mousseline : mince the fish twice and
put it into a bowl or mixer, then
work well, gradually adding
the egg whites. Pass mixture
through a wire sieve, return
it to the bowl and gradually stir
in the cream. Season mousseline
and set it aside.

To prepare the prawn
butter : remove the head and
tail shells from the prawns,
reserving about 6-8 prawns
for the garnish. Pound or blend
the flesh and shells with the
butter, pass mixture through a
wire sieve, then set aside.

Set oven at 425°F or Mark 7.
To make bouchées : roll out
pastry to ½ inch thick, stamp out
6-8 rounds with larger cutter and
lift onto a dampened baking
sheet. Lightly brush rounds with
egg wash and with smaller
cutter mark centre of each one.
Chill for a few minutes and
bake for 15-20 minutes in pre-set
oven, or until golden brown.
With the point of a small knife,
lift out the centre lid and scoop
out any soft centre.

After baking bouchées reduce
oven to 350°F or Mark 4. Wash
and dry salmon steak, place in
ovenproof dish with water and
lemon juice, then poach for 30
minutes in oven. Remove skin
and bones and flake flesh.
Sauté the mushrooms in the
butter.

To make quenelles : use 2
dessertspoons to shape the
salmon mousseline into small
ovals. Lift them into a large
shallow pan of boiling salted
water, reduce heat so that water
is barely simmering and poach
for 10-12 minutes or until firm
to the touch ; drain them carefully, arrange on a hot serving
dish and keep warm.

Prepare the Nantua sauce as
for a white sauce and finish
by stirring in the cream (or
creamy milk) and prawn butter.
Mix a small quantity of this
sauce with the flaked salmon
and mushrooms and fill the
bouchées. Garnish each one
with reserved prawns.

Coat the quenelles with remaining Nantua sauce and
arrange the bouchées around
the dish.

Smoked salmon rolls with prawns

8 oz smoked salmon (8-10 good slices)
10 oz shelled prawns (frozen)
good $\frac{1}{4}$ pint thick mayonnaise
3-4 drops of Tabasco sauce
$\frac{1}{2}$ teaspoon paprika pepper
$\frac{1}{2}$ teaspoon tomato purée
1 dessertspoon double cream (optional)

To serve
8 wedges of lemon
brown bread and butter

Method

Leave salmon in the paper in which it was bought, and roughly chop prawns. Blend mayonnaise with Tabasco sauce, paprika pepper, tomato purée and cream, if used. Bind the prawns together with the mayonnaise and divide the mixture among the slices of salmon. Place one portion on each salmon slice and roll up. Dish up on individual plates, with a wedge of lemon on each.

Serve with brown bread and butter, and provide a small fork for easy eating.

Using forks to roll up a slice of smoked salmon with prawn and mayonnaise filling

Salmon steaks au gourmet

3 salmon steaks (each weighing
  6-8 oz)
1 wineglass white wine
squeeze of lemon juice
1 slice of onion
6 peppercorns
sprig of parsley

For hollandaise sauce
4 tablespoons tarragon vinegar
1 blade of mace
6 peppercorns
3 egg yolks (beaten)
4-6 oz butter

For garnish
3 tomatoes
3 oz button mushrooms
$\frac{1}{2}$ oz butter
salt and pepper
tomato purée
grated rind of $\frac{1}{2}$ orange

This recipe serves 6 for a first
course. If serving as a main
course for 4, use 2 salmon
steaks, each weighing 8-12 oz.

Method

Wash and dry salmon steaks.
Set oven at 350°F or Mark 4.
Place steaks in an ovenproof
dish and poach them in the
white wine and lemon juice,
with onion and seasonings, in
pre-set moderate oven for about
15 minutes.

To prepare hollandaise sauce :
reduce tarragon vinegar with
the mace and peppercorns.
Cream the egg yolk with $\frac{1}{4}$ oz
butter ; strain and add the
liquid. Thicken sauce in a bain-
marie, gradually adding remaining butter. Set sauce aside.

To prepare the garnish : scald
and skin tomatoes, cut in four,
squeeze away the seeds and cut
flesh into neat shreds. Slice the
mushrooms and sauté in butter,
with a squeeze of lemon juice
and seasoning.

Strain the liquor from the fish,
reduce it to 1 tablespoon and
add it to hollandaise sauce with
a 'touch' of tomato purée, and
the orange rind. Remove the
skin and bones from the salmon,
divide each steak in two and
arrange in a warm serving dish.
Add the garnish to the sauce
and spoon it over the fish.
This may be glazed quickly
under a hot grill, if wished,
before serving.

Salmon Koulibiac

12 oz quantity of puff pastry
egg wash
sprigs of watercress
$\frac{1}{2}$ pint mock hollandaise sauce

For filling
1 lb fresh salmon (poached)
salt and pepper
lemon juice
$\frac{1}{4}$ lb mushrooms
6 spring onions
2-3 oz butter
2 eggs (hard-boiled)
6 oz long grain rice (boiled)

This is a classic Russian dish.

Method

Remove the skin and bones from poached salmon and flake into a bowl ; season with salt, pepper and lemon juice. Wash the mushrooms in salted water, dry and slice them. Trim and chop the spring onions and put in a pan with half the butter ; cook them slowly for 1 minute, then add the mushrooms and simmer for 5 minutes. Melt the remaining butter. Chop the eggs and add them to the salmon with the rice, mushroom mixture and remaining melted butter. Taste for seasoning.

Set oven at 400°F or Mark 6. Roll out puff pastry into a rectangle, cut off a 1-inch wide strip for fleurons ; cut off two-thirds of the remaining pastry, put the salmon mixture on this larger piece and' fold the pastry around it. Lay the other piece of pastry over the top, seal edges, brush with egg wash and decorate with fleurons, bake in pre-set oven for about 25-30 minutes. Garnish with watercress and serve mock hollandaise sauce separately.

Salmon trout en gelée

$2\frac{1}{2}$-3 lb salmon trout
$1\frac{1}{2}$ pints court bouillon
aspic (made from fish liquor, see method)

For mayonnaise Nantua
3 oz shrimps, or prawns (with shells)
$\frac{1}{2}$ pint oil
$\frac{1}{2}$ teaspoon paprika pepper
2-3 egg yolks
salt and pepper
$1\frac{1}{2}$-2 dessertspoons white wine vinegar

For garnish
$\frac{1}{2}$ pint prawns
$\frac{1}{2}$ cucumber
1 bunch of watercress

Method

First make the court bouillon and set aside. Trim trout and vandyke the tail. Wash fish well, taking care to scrape away the blood that lies against the backbone and to remove the gills (this may have been done by the fishmonger). Slightly curl the fish and place it, underside down, in a fish kettle or oven-proof dish and pour over the well-seasoned court bouillon, while it is still warm. Poach fish for 25-30 minutes in a fish kettle, or poach in the oven, for 35-45 minutes (set oven at 350°F or Mark 4). On no account must the liquid around the fish boil, and if poaching fish in oven baste it frequently.

Allow the fish to cool in the court bouillon, then lift it carefully on to a board or large dish. Use absorbent paper to remove any specks of fat floating on the surface of fish stock and strain it into a clean, scalded pan, ready for making the aspic.

Salmon trout en gelée

Prepare aspic and allow to cool (see page 58).

Snip skin along top of trout and remove it carefully, leaving head and tail intact. Cut through the backbone just below head and ease knife along the bone ; gently lift bone up and out towards the tail ; cut it just short of the tail and discard it.

Run a little cool aspic over the serving dish and leave it to set. Lift the trout, using a fish slice and palette knife for support and place it on the prepared dish.

To prepare mayonnaise Nantua : shell the shrimps, or prawns. Pound the shells with the paprika in the oil and leave to soak for 10-15 minutes. Chop the prawns roughly, or leave shrimps whole, and strain oil. Prepare mayonnaise in the usual way, adding shrimps or prawns.

Slice the cucumber finely ; peel the tail shells from the prawns but do not remove their heads. Arrange the prawns along the top of the fish and then baste with cold liquid aspic. Decorate the dish with the cucumber and watercress and serve with mayonnaise Nantua, and new potatoes, tossed in melted butter and chopped parsley.

After snipping skin along top of trout it can be carefully peeled off. Having cut through backbone below head, ease knife along and remove backbone gently

Right : The finished salmon trout, garnished with cucumber slices, prawns, watercress and chopped aspic, is served with mayonnaise Nantua

Salmon trout with fennel

2-3 lb salmon trout

For court bouillon
1 onion (sliced)
2 carrots (sliced)
1 stick of celery (sliced)
1 large bouquet garni
6 peppercorns
juice of $\frac{1}{2}$ lemon
1 pint water

For garnish
1 large cucumber (peeled and
  sliced)
1 oz butter
salt and pepper
1 dessertspoon chopped fennel,
  or dill

For butter sauce
1 shallot, or small onion (finely
  chopped)
2 wineglasses white wine
2 egg yolks (beaten)
3 oz butter

For velouté sauce
1 oz butter
1 oz plain flour
$\frac{1}{2}$-$\frac{3}{4}$ pint chicken stock
salt and pepper

To finish
$2\frac{1}{2}$ fl oz double cream
1 dessertspoon chopped fennel,
  or dill

Method

Trim, wash and dry the trout.
Set oven at 325-350°F or Mark
3-4. Put the ingredients for
court bouillon in a pan and
simmer for 10 minutes. Place
trout in an ovenproof dish
and pour over the court
bouillon. Poach in a pre-set
slow to moderate oven for
40-45 minutes (basting fish
occasionally).

Meanwhile prepare garnish :
peel cucumber, cut into pieces
and blanch in boiling water.
Drain and return cucumber to
the pan with the butter and
seasoning ; cover pan and cook
gently for 4-5 minutes. Finish
with the fennel (or dill) and set
aside.

To prepare butter sauce : add
the shallot (or onion) to the
wine and reduce it by half.
Cream the egg yolks with $\frac{1}{4}$ oz
butter ; strain and add the liquid.
Thicken sauce in a bain-marie,
gradually adding the rest of the
butter, then set it aside.

To make velouté sauce : melt
butter, add flour and cook until
a pale straw colour. Blend in
the chicken stock off the heat,
return to stove and bring to
boil ; cook 3-4 minutes. Remove
from heat, beat in the butter
sauce, cream and fennel (or
dill). Adjust seasoning and keep
sauce warm. Take up trout, skin
it carefully and dish up. Coat
with some of the sauce and
serve the rest separately.
Garnish the dish with the
cucumber slices.

Salmon trout vin rosé

1 salmon trout (weighing
  2-2$\frac{1}{2}$ lb)
4 shallots, or 1 medium-size
  onion (finely chopped)
$\frac{1}{2}$-$\frac{3}{4}$ bottle vin rosé
1 wineglass water

For sauce
$\frac{1}{2}$ oz butter
$\frac{1}{2}$ oz plain flour
4 tablespoons double cream
salt and pepper
$\frac{1}{4}$ pint hollandaise (made with
  2 egg yolks, 3-4 tablespoons
  wine vinegar, mace, peppercorns, bayleaf, 4 oz butter) —
  see page 48

For garnish
1 cucumber
1 bunch of spring onions
1 oz butter
1 teaspoon chopped parsley
triangular croûtes of bread
butter (for frying)

Method

Set oven at 300°F or Mark 2.

Trim trout, place it in well-buttered ovenproof dish, add the shallots, wine and water. Poach in pre-set slow oven for 40-45 minutes. Take up, strain the liquid into a pan and reduce by about a third. Skin the trout and keep warm.

To make sauce : melt butter in a pan, stir in the flour, then pour on the reduced liquid. Stir until boiling, add cream and seasoning, then simmer for a few minutes. Draw pan aside. Have ready the hollandaise and beat this into the sauce.

To make the garnish : peel the cucumber, cut it in half length-ways and then again into $\frac{1}{2}$-inch slices. Trim the spring onions and cut into 1-inch lengths. Blanch onions and cucumber in boiling salted water for 2-3 minutes, drain well and return to the pan with the butter and seasoning. Simmer for 3-5 minutes until tender and finish with a teaspoon of chopped parsley. Fry the croûtes in butter until golden-brown. Dish up the trout, coat with some of the sauce and serve the rest separately. Surround the dish with croûtes and garnish with cucumber and spring onions.

Stuffed fish

two 1$\frac{1}{2}$ lb, or one 3$\frac{1}{2}$ lb, fish
$\frac{1}{4}$ pint sherry
$\frac{1}{4}$ pint milk

For stuffing
$\frac{1}{2}$ small onion (chopped)
2 tablespoons melted butter
3 oz white breadcrumbs
$\frac{1}{2}$ teaspoon salt
pepper (ground from mill)
1 tablespoon chopped parsley
pinch of dried mixed herbs
2 tablespoons hot water

In New Zealand trout are really the finest fish and are caught in many of the lakes and rivers on both islands. This recipe is quite excellent for our own sea trout and would do for any whole, firm, round fish.

Method

Wash and dry the fish very well, and if it has only been cleaned through the gills by the fishmonger, slit it down the belly. Wash and clean this cavity very well and dry thoroughly. Then place the fish in a casserole, pour over the sherry, cover and leave in the refrigerator overnight.

Set the oven at 350°F or Mark 4. To prepare the stuffing : soften the onion in the butter and add it to the crumbs. Add the seasoning, parsley, herbs and hot water. Place the stuffing in the fish, pour over the milk, season and bake in the pre-set moderate oven 35-40 minutes for a 3$\frac{1}{2}$ lb fish or 20-25 minutes for a 1$\frac{1}{2}$ lb dish. Serve this hot or cold.

Stuffed trout Nantua

4-5 even-size trout
court bouillon (for poaching)

For prawn mousse
8 oz prawns (shelled)
$\frac{1}{4}$ pint thick béchamel sauce
2 oz butter (creamed)
salt and pepper
2 tablespoons double cream
(partially whipped)
$\frac{1}{2}$ pint mayonnaise
pinch of paprika pepper
$\frac{1}{2}$ teaspoon Tabasco sauce, or
1-2 tablespoons tomato juice
cocktail

For garnish
$\frac{1}{2}$ cucumber and sprigs of watercress, or extra prawns

Method
Poach the trout in court bouillon
and leave to cool. Remove skin
and bones.

To prepare prawn mousse :
mince prawns and pound them
with the cold béchamel sauce,
or work together in a blender.
Add the creamed butter, adjust
the seasoning and fold in the
cream.

Stuff each trout with the
prawn mixture and arrange on
a serving dish. Season the
mayonnaise with paprika and
Tabasco sauce (or tomato juice
cocktail) and spoon a little
over each trout ; hand the
remainder separately.

For garnish : slice or dice the
cucumber, sprinkle with salt
and press between two plates.
Drain off any liquid after 30
minutes, then arrange cucumber around dish with watercress
(or prawns).

Trout Genève

4-5 trout
4 oz mushrooms (quartered)
6 oz butter
2 shallots (finely chopped)
$3\frac{1}{2}$ oz stale bread (made into
breadcrumbs)
2 lemons
1 lb potatoes (shaped in balls
the size of marbles)

For court bouillon
2 wineglasses white wine
1 bouquet garni
1 carrot (sliced)
1 onion (sliced)
salt and pepper

Method
Trim, wash and dry the trout.
Make the court bouillon ; when
it is tepid poach the trout in this
for 10-15 minutes. Then drain
and skin fish, place them in a
serving dish and keep warm.

Sauté the mushrooms and
shallots in 1 oz of butter, then
set aside.

Strain the court bouillon,
gradually add the crumbs to it
and simmer for 5 minutes. Then
add a good ounce of butter in
small pieces, the mushrooms,
a good squeeze of lemon juice
and season. Spoon this sauce
over the trout and garnish the
dish with lemon slices. Brown
the potatoes until golden in
remaining butter and serve
around the fish.

Trout à la genevoise

5-6 small, even-size trout
salt
1 wineglass water
4-6 peppercorns
1½ lb potatoes (cut into small
   balls and plainly boiled)

For sauce
1 small onion (finely chopped)
1 small carrot (finely chopped)
1 oz butter
2 wineglasses red wine
kneaded butter (made with ¾
   oz butter and ½ oz flour)
salt and pepper
a dash of anchovy essence
a little thyme (chopped)
1 dessertspoon chopped parsley

Method
Set the oven at 350°F or Mark 4
and clean and trim the trout as
usual. Butter an ovenproof dish
well, lay in the trout and add a
little salt, the water and peppercorns. Cover with a buttered
paper and poach for about 15
minutes in the pre-set moderate
oven.

To make the sauce : sauté the
onion and carrot in ½ oz of the
butter, then add the wine and
simmer until reduced to half
quantity. Strain off the liquor
from the trout and add to the
pan. Simmer for 4-5 minutes,
thicken slightly with kneaded
butter, reboil, adjust seasoning
and add the anchovy essence,
thyme, remaining butter and
chopped parsley. Spoon sauce
over trout ; serve potato balls at
each end of dish.

*Straining liquor from trout into the
sauce*

Trout à la genevoise has a sauce with red wine, onions, carrots, herbs and a dash of anchovy sauce

River trout en gelée

5-6 even-size trout
$7\frac{1}{2}$ fl oz white wine, or white
   wine and water (for poaching)
salt and pepper
1 pint good fish stock (see page 60)
$1\frac{1}{4}$ oz gelatine
1 wineglass white wine
1 wineglass sherry
1 egg white
mayonnaise (optional)

For garnish
6 small, even-size ripe tomatoes
$\frac{1}{4}$ lb shelled shrimps
2-3 tablespoons thick
   mayonnaise
1 bundle of small asparagus, or
   sprue

Method

Set the oven at 325°F or Mark 3. Trim, wash and dry the trout, lay in an ovenproof dish, pour over the white wine (or wine and water), season lightly and poach in the pre-set oven for 20-25 minutes, or until the eyes of the fish turn white. Baste fish occasionally. Take them up, cool, then lift on to a wire rack or tray.

Strain off the liquor in which trout were poached and measure $\frac{1}{2}$ pint. Add this to the fish stock; there should be $1\frac{1}{2}$ pints in all. Turn this into a large scalded pan and use with gelatine, wines and egg white to prepare aspic (see method page 58).

Now prepare the garnish. Scald the tomatoes, cut off the tops at the flower end, scoop out the seeds and fill the tomatoes with the shrimps, bound with a little mayonnaise. Cook the asparagus (or sprue) and divide into 5-6 bundles.

Skin the trout, cool a little of the aspic, then brush or coat the trout with this. Make sure that there is a good coating. Run a little cool aspic on to a silver, or steel, dish and, when set, lift the trout carefully onto this. Coat the little bundles of asparagus with cool aspic and set each on a trout. Surround with tomatoes and garnish in between with croûtons of aspic. Chill slightly before serving and, if wished, a sauce boat of mayonnaise may be handed separately.

Trout Barbizon

4-5 river trout
$\frac{3}{4}$ lb tomatoes
1 dessertspoon tomato purée
1 clove of garlic
salt and pepper
seasoned flour
butter (for frying)
1 tablespoon finely chopped
    onion
1 pinch of saffron (soaked for
    30 minutes in 2-3 tablespoons
    hot water)
$\frac{1}{4}$ pint double cream

Method
Cut and squeeze tomatoes to remove the seeds ; cook them to a pulp with tomato purée and garlic, season well, strain and set aside.

Trim the trout and roll them in seasoned flour. Fry them slowly in plenty of butter until they are golden-brown, then dish up and keep warm.

Add the onion to the pan and cook slowly until it is golden, adding a little extra butter, if necessary. Then add the tomato pulp, saffron liquid, cream and season. Stir sauce well and bring it to boil, pour over the trout and serve.

Pancakes Beatrix

For batter
$3\frac{1}{2}$ oz plain flour
pinch of salt
2 eggs
2 tablespoons melted butter, or
    salad oil
$\frac{1}{4}$-$\frac{1}{2}$ pint milk
1 oz Gouda cheese (finely grated)

For filling
2-3 smoked trout
béchamel sauce (made with 1 oz
    butter, 1 oz flour, $\frac{1}{2}$ pint flavoured
    milk)
salt and pepper
1 teaspoon horseradish cream
1 tablespoon double cream

For finishing
3 tablespoons double cream
1 tablespoon grated Parmesan
    cheese

Method
Sift the flour with the salt into a bowl, make a well in the centre, add the eggs and begin to add the milk slowly, stirring all the time. When half the milk has been added, stir in the butter, or oil, and cheese and beat well until smooth. Add remaining milk. Leave to stand for 30 minutes in a cool place.

Remove the skin and bone from the trout and divide into neat fillets. Make béchamel sauce, season, then add the horseradish cream and table-spoon of double cream.

Set the oven at 375°F or Mark 5. Fry paper-thin pan-cakes, fill each one with the fillets and sauce, roll up like cigars and arrange in a buttered dish. Spoon over the extra cream, dust with Parmesan cheese and bake in the pre-set oven for about 10 minutes.

Tunny fish mousse

3 cans tunny fish (about 21 oz)
cold béchamel sauce (made with
   $1\frac{1}{2}$ oz butter, $1\frac{1}{2}$ oz flour, 1 pint
   flavoured milk)
$\frac{1}{2}$ pint mayonnaise
1 oz gelatine
$\frac{1}{4}$ pint vegetable stock, or water
salt and pepper
2 egg whites (stiffly whisked)

To garnish
1 small cucumber, or 1 head of
   celery
$\frac{1}{2}$ lb tomatoes
French dressing
1 teaspoon chopped mint

Ring mould ($2\frac{1}{2}$ pints capacity)

Method
Lightly oil the mould.
   Drain the fish and pound
with the cold béchamel sauce
until smooth, then work in the
mayonnaise. Soak and dissolve
the gelatine in the stock (or
water) and add to the mixture,
season well. As the mixture
begins to thicken, fold in the
egg whites. Turn mousse into
the mould and leave to set.
   Peel the cucumber ; cut into
thick julienne strips, salt them
lightly, cover and leave for 30
minutes, then drain. Or wash
celery ; cut in julienne strips.
   Scald and skin the tomatoes,
cut in four and scoop away the
seeds. Mix the cucumber (or
celery) and tomatoes together,
moisten with French dressing
and add the mint. Turn the
mousse out of mould and fill
the centre with the salad.

Eggs with tunny fish

3 eggs (hard-boiled)
3-4 tablespoons tunny fish, or
   1 small can (flaked)
$1\frac{1}{2}$ oz creamed butter, or 1
   tablespoon mayonnaise
salt and pepper

For béchamel sauce
$\frac{1}{4}$ pint milk (infused with 1 bayleaf,
   1 blade of mace and 6 pepper-
   corns)
$\frac{1}{2}$ oz butter
scant $\frac{1}{2}$ oz plain flour

For salad
$\frac{1}{4}$ lb French beans
4 oz black olives (stoned)
$\frac{1}{2}$ lb firm tomatoes (skinned,
   quartered and seeds removed)
French dressing (lightly
   flavoured with garlic)

This makes a good party dish
for a first course or one for a
summer lunch. Other fish or
meat, chicken and ham, can be
used instead of tunny fish.

Method
First prepare béchamel sauce ;
make a roux of melted butter and
flour, strain on the flavoured
milk, stir until boiling. Set aside
to cool.
   Peel and halve the eggs.
Sieve the yolks, then pound
them in a basin with the tunny
fish, 3 tablespoons béchamel
sauce, and creamed butter or
mayonnaise. Season well.
   Wash and dry the egg whites,
arrange round a serving dish,
securing them with a little of
the mixture. Put the remaining
mixture into a forcing bag
fitted with a plain nozzle and
pipe into the whites.
   Mix the salad ingredients
together and pile into the centre.

Tarte au poisson

For rich shortcrust pastry
8 oz plain flour
4 oz butter
1 oz shortening
1 egg yolk
2-3 tablespoons water (to mix)

For filling
7 oz can tunny fish (flaked)
4 tomatoes
1 oz butter
2-3 onions (finely sliced)
$\frac{1}{2}$ oz plain flour
$\frac{1}{4}$ pint milk
salt and pepper
grated nutmeg
2 eggs (beaten)
2 oz grated cheese

8-inch diameter flan ring

Method
First prepare the rich shortcrust pastry and chill. Roll out pastry and line into a plain or fluted flan ring and bake blind for about 15 minutes. Meanwhile scald and skin tomatoes, cut in half, remove seeds, and set flesh on one side.

Melt the butter in a pan, add the onions and cook until soft. Mix in the flour and add the milk. Stir sauce until boiling, draw aside and add seasoning, nutmeg, and beaten eggs. Arrange the tomatoes and flaked tunny fish in the bottom of the flan, season, and pour in the sauce to fill well.

Scatter with grated cheese and put into the oven, pre-set at 350°F or Mark 4, until well set and golden-brown (about 30 minutes). Serve warm.

Mackerel algérienne

4 mackerel
salt and pepper
$\frac{1}{2}$ lemon
chopped parsley

For salpicon
1 red, or green, pepper
$\frac{3}{4}$ lb tomatoes
$\frac{1}{2}$ oz butter
1 shallot (finely chopped)
1 clove of garlic (crushed with
   $\frac{1}{4}$ teaspoon salt)
1 teaspoon paprika pepper

Method
Set oven at 350°F or Mark 4.

First split and bone the mackerel, wash and dry well. Place the fish in an ovenproof dish, season and squeeze over a little lemon juice. Bake in pre-set oven for about 20 minutes.

To prepare the salpicon: shred the pepper, blanch and refresh. Skin the tomatoes, remove seeds and slice flesh. Melt the butter, add the shallot and cook until soft. Then add the tomatoes, garlic and paprika pepper. Stew slowly to a pulp, then add the pepper ; continue cooking for 2-3 minutes.

Spoon salpicon over the fish and serve with thin slices of lemon and chopped parsley.

Devilled sardines

2 cans (4 oz each) sardines
½ oz butter
salt and pepper
grated rind of ½ lemon and
  juice of 1 lemon
1 tablespoon tomato ketchup,
  or tomato chutney
1 dessertspoon mushroom
  ketchup, or Worcestershire sauce
little dry mustard
1 dessertspoon chopped mixed
  herbs
4-5 rounds of hot toast
  (buttered) — for serving

Method
Open the cans of sardines,
drain off the oil and turn the fish
on to a plate. Pour over ½ cup
boiling water to wash off any
remaining oil and tilt the plate
to drain thoroughly.

Heat a pan, put in the butter
and slide in the sardines. Season
well and add the remaining
ingredients. Heat until bubbling.
Have the rounds of toast ready
and arrange the sardines on
them, using a slice.

Sardine salad

1 large can sardines
1 small onion
1 lb tomatoes
2 tablespoons capers
4 tablespoons French dressing
1 tablespoon chopped parsley

Method
Drain the sardines, split, and
remove the centre bones. Grate
onion ; scald, skin and slice the
tomatoes.

Put a layer of sliced tomatoes
in an entrée dish, sprinkle half
the grated onion and half the
capers over them and cover
with a layer of sardines. Arrange
the remaining tomatoes in a
layer on top, cover with the
rest of the onion, capers and
sardines. Spoon the French
dressing over all and dust top
with chopped parsley.

Shellfish

Shellfish are the real delicacies of the fish world. In some countries it is because they are so plentiful and delicious ; in Britain they are more scarce and all the more delicious.

Freshness is the key to a good shellfish of any kind. It is much the best if you can obtain your fish while it is still alive and kill it yourself. This is not as difficult as it sounds — you don't have to send your family out at night to sit over their own lobster pots. Many fishmongers, even inland, display lobsters and crabs still walking around the slab ; if this is the case, choose one that is good and lively and you are half way to a delicious meal. If you can't find a supply of live fish, be sure that the one you buy is fresh from the market the same day and you cannot go far wrong.

There are some shellfish that are so rare on our shores that we have to import. Scampi is one of these, arriving frozen from the Adriatic ; Dublin Bay prawns are also usually frozen. The rule with these is to thaw them slowly and thoroughly at refrigerator temperature and then to eat them immediately ; decay sets in very quickly once frozen food is thawed. Fresh oysters are another luxury we can rarely afford here ; if they are obtainable they are usually considered such a delicacy that they are eaten raw. The cook more often than not has to be content with canned oysters — which are certainly ideal for the soup on page 130.

Crab salad printanier

1 medium-size crab, or 8 oz crab
  meat (frozen, or canned)
4 globe artichokes, or canned
  artichoke 'fonds'
2 tablespoons French dressing
rind and juice of 1 orange
2 oz black olives (stoned)
$\frac{1}{2}$ pint mayonnaise
4 large lettuce leaves

Method

Trim the artichokes and cook
them in boiling, salted water
for 45 minutes or until a leaf
can be pulled out easily. Drain
and refresh them. Pull out the
centre leaves carefully, scrape
away the choke and then remove
each leaf, one by one, and
discard. Spoon the French
dressing over the hearts and
leave them to marinate until
cold.

Remove a strip of orange rind
with a potato peeler, cut it in
fine shreds and cook for 2-3
minutes in boiling water until
tender ; then drain. Grate a little
of the remaining orange rind.

Watchpoint The rind must be
grated on the very finest side
of the grater (nutmeg grater) ;
make sure that only the zest is
used and none of the pith.

Flavour the mayonnaise to
taste with a little strained orange
juice and the finely grated
orange rind.

Arrange the lettuce leaves
on individual salad plates, place
an artichoke heart on top and
cover with crab meat ; spoon
over the mayonnaise. Garnish
with shredded orange rind and
olives, and serve with brown
bread and butter.

*Carefully removing the outer leaves
of the cooked artichoke ; the centre
leaves and the choke have already
been pulled out*

Aubergine with crab

2 good-size aubergines
6-7 oz crab claw meat
salt and pepper
oil
2 medium-size onions
1 dessertspoon paprika pepper
1 tablespoon tomato purée
½ lb ripe tomatoes (skinned, seeds
   removed, and sliced)
½ teaspoon oregano
pinch of cayenne pepper, or drop
   of Tabasco sauce
2 tablespoons grated Parmesan
   and Gruyère cheese (mixed)
1-2 tablespoons melted butter

Method

Split aubergines in two lengthways, score, sprinkle with salt and leave for 30 minutes. Set oven at 350°F or Mark 4.

Wipe aubergines dry, then brown the cut surface in a little hot oil ; take out, set on a baking tin and cook in pre-set moderate oven until tender (about 10 minutes).

Meanwhile slice onions and soften in 2-3 tablespoons oil ; add paprika and after a few seconds add tomato purée, tomatoes, oregano and cayenne (or Tabasco). Season and cook to a rich pulp. Scoop out the pulp from the cooked aubergines, add it to the pan and continue to cook for a few minutes. Then flake the crab meat with a fork and add it to the pan. Pile this mixture into the aubergine skins, sprinkle well with cheese and melted butter and bake in quick oven (425°F or Mark 7) for 6-7 minutes to brown.

Crab mousse

1 lb crab meat ($\frac{1}{2}$ white, $\frac{1}{2}$ dark)
$\frac{1}{2}$ pint velouté sauce (made with
1 oz butter, 1 oz flour, $\frac{1}{2}$ pint court
bouillon, or light chicken stock —
see method, page 19)
$\frac{1}{2}$ oz gelatine
$2\frac{1}{2}$ fl oz white wine
$\frac{1}{2}$ pint mayonnaise
$\frac{1}{4}$ pint double cream (lightly whipped)

For garnish
1 cucumber
4 tablespoons French dressing
$\frac{1}{2}$ teaspoon paprika pepper
Tabasco sauce

*7-inch diameter top (No. 1 size)
soufflé dish, or cake tin*

Method
Oil the dish or tin. Prepare the
velouté sauce, work in the dark
crab meat and leave to cool.
Soak the gelatine in wine, dissolve it over heat and then stir it
into velouté sauce with the
mayonnaise. Fold the flaked
white crab meat into the mixture
with the cream. Turn mousse into
the prepared dish or tin and
leave it to set.

Meanwhile, slice the cucumber, and dégorge. Flavour the
French dressing with paprika
and a good dash of Tabasco
and mix with cucumber. Turn
mousse on to a serving dish and
spoon cucumber over it.

Crab armoricaine

1 lb crab meat
1 onion (finely chopped)
1 oz butter
$\frac{1}{4}$ lb mushrooms (chopped)
1 tablespoon brandy
3 tablespoons thick fresh tomato
pulp (see page 40)
$\frac{1}{2}$ wineglass white wine
salt, pepper, cayenne pepper and a
pinch of curry powder
1 tablespoon browned breadcrumbs

Method
Soften the onion in the butter
without letting it colour, add
the chopped mushrooms and
continue to cook for 3-5
minutes. Then add the brandy,
tomato pulp, wine and seasoning and stir in the crab meat.
Turn the mixture into the crab
shell or a gratin dish, dust with
the crumbs and sprinkle with a
little melted butter. Brown under
the grill or in a quick oven at
425°F or Mark 7.

Crab croquettes

½ lb crab meat (white and dark mixed)
¼ pint béchamel sauce (made with 1 oz butter, 1 scant oz flour and ¼ pint flavoured milk)
1 small egg
Tabasco sauce (to taste)
salt and pepper

For coating
seasoned flour
1 egg (beaten)
dried white breadcrumbs

Deep fat bath

Method
Prepare the béchamel sauce in the usual way and leave until cold. Beat in the crab meat, egg, Tabasco sauce and seasoning. Shape the mixture into large marbles, and roll these in seasoned flour, beaten egg and crumbs. Fry in deep fat until golden. Serve very hot with mustard sauce.

Lobster boréale

1 live lobster (1-1½ lb)
2 pints court bouillon
2 oz butter

For fish mousseline
¾ lb hake
2 egg whites (lightly beaten)
¼ pint double cream
salt and white pepper
3 tablespoons milk

For béchamel sauce
1 oz butter
¾ oz plain flour
8 fl oz flavoured milk

For garnish
2 oz mushrooms
½ oz butter
salt and pepper
½ pint shrimps (cooked)
4 hard-boiled eggs

Method
First make the mousseline. Set the oven at 350°F or Mark 4. Mince the raw hake and beat in the egg whites a little at a time, then rub the mixture through a wire sieve. Add the cream gradually and season well, then add the milk. Put the mixture in a buttered ovenproof dish and poach in the pre-set oven for 15-20 minutes.

Meanwhile rinse the lobster in cold water, put into boiling court bouillon and cook for 30 minutes. Remove the lobster shell and cut the tail meat in thick scallops. Pound the coral or spawn with 2 oz butter and rub through a strainer to make lobster butter.

Prepare the béchamel sauce in the usual way and beat in the lobster butter. Dilute the sauce with a little of the court bouillon, if necessary.

Now make the garnish. Wash

and trim the mushrooms, slice finely and cook in the butter, with seasoning, for 1 minute. Mix the shrimps and the mushrooms together. Cut the eggs in half, remove the yolks and rub these through a sieve. Fill the egg whites with the shrimp and mushroom salpicon.

To dish up, turn the fish mousse on to a flat, oval serving dish. Arrange the scallops of lobster overlapping on the top and spoon over the lobster sauce. Arrange the stuffed eggs around the dish and sprinkle on the sieved egg yolk. Decorate the dish with the lobster shell split in half and lightly brushed with oil.

Lobster bisque

1 medium-size live lobster
3 oz butter
2 tablespoons oil
1 small onion (finely chopped)
1 wineglass sherry
2 pints fish stock

For velouté
$1\frac{1}{2}$ oz butter
$1\frac{1}{2}$ oz plain flour
salt and pepper
$\frac{1}{4}$ pint double cream

If wished, a can of lobster claw meat may be used for this soup, but to get the very best flavour you should make it with a live lobster.

Method
If you have a live lobster, kill and split it ; remove the bag from the head (discard this) and the coral.

Make lobster butter by working the coral with $1\frac{1}{2}$ oz of the butter. Set this mixture aside.

Heat the oil and $1\frac{1}{2}$ oz of the butter in a large sauté pan. Put the lobster in the pan, cover and cook for 5 minutes, then add the onion and the sherry. Cover and simmer for 10-15 minutes. Take up, remove all the meat from the body and claws. **Note :** if wished, some of the tail meat may be reserved for garnish, in which case cut it in slices and add to the soup just before serving.

Pound the meat or work it in an electric blender with a little of the stock.

Now prepare the velouté : melt the butter, stir in the flour, pour on the stock and any juices from the lobster pan. Bring to the boil, season and simmer for 5-6 minutes ; draw aside. Add the pounded lobster and the lobster butter in small pieces and reheat, adding the cream, but do not allow to boil. Serve at once.

Lobster Margareta

2 lobsters (1 lb each)
2 pints court bouillon
1 shallot (finely chopped)
$\frac{1}{2}$ oz butter
1 glass sherry
6 oz mushrooms (sliced)
squeeze of lemon juice
salt and pepper
4 tomatoes (skinned and
    quartered)
2 tablespoons double cream

For sauce
2 egg yolks
salt and pepper
1 teaspoon French mustard
$\frac{1}{2}$ pint salad oil
lemon juice
1 teaspoon chopped mixed parsley,
    tarragon and chervil
4 tomatoes (skinned and quartered),
    or 1 teaspoon tomato purée
small pinch of cayenne pepper
dash of Worcestershire sauce

To kill a lobster without boiling it : choose a sharp chopping knife. Lay the lobster out flat on a wooden board, hard shell uppermost. Have the head toward your right hand and cover the tail with a cloth. Hold lobster firmly behind the head with your left hand and with the point of the knife pierce right through the little cross mark which lies on the centre of the head. The lobster is killed at once.

Method

Rinse the lobster in cold water and put into boiling court bouillon. Cook for 20-30 minutes, cool a little in the liquid, then drain and set aside. Cook the shallot in the butter until soft but not coloured, add the sherry and simmer until reduced to half quantity, then add the mushrooms and lemon juice. Season and cook quickly for 3-4 minutes, then add the tomatoes and cream. Cook for a further 3 minutes and taste for seasoning. Allow to cool.

Split the lobsters, remove the tail meat and cut into scallops. Remove the shell from the claws, keeping meat as whole as possible. Put the mushroom mixture in the bottom of each shell, arrange the lobster meat on the top, placing the claw meat in the head shell.

Prepare a mayonnaise with the egg yolks, seasoning and mustard, oil and lemon juice, then add the herbs. Remove the seeds from the tomatoes and chop the flesh quite finely. Add this (or the tomato purée) to the mayonnaise. Season with the cayenne and Worcestershire sauce, adding an extra squeeze of lemon juice if necessary. Coat the lobster with just enough sauce to cover and serve the rest separately. Arrange on a serving dish and garnish with watercress. Serve with cold, plainly boiled rice mixed with French dressing.

Lobster tartlets
(bateaux de homard)

4 oz quantity savoury shortcrust
   pastry (baked in 12-16 boat
   moulds)
3-4 oz cooked lobster (fresh or
   canned)
French dressing
chopped celery (about half
   quantity of lobster)
1 teaspoon chopped parsley
1-2 tablespoons thick
   mayonnaise
2 tablespoons chopped
   watercress

Method
Cut the lobster meat into small
pieces and leave to soak in a
little French dressing while
baking the boat moulds of
savoury shortcrust pastry.

Drain the lobster and mix it
with the celery and parsley,
and add just enough mayonnaise to bind the mixture together. Fill it into the boat
moulds and cover the top with
the chopped watercress.

Lobster mousse

1 large live lobster (weight
   about 2 lb)
2 pints court bouillon (for
   cooking lobster)
$\frac{1}{2}$ pint velouté sauce (made with
   1 oz butter, 1 oz flour, $\frac{1}{2}$ pint
   court bouillon in which
   lobster has been cooked — see
   method, page 19)
$\frac{1}{2}$ oz gelatine
3 eggs (hard-boiled)
$7\frac{1}{2}$ fl oz mayonnaise
$2\frac{1}{2}$ fl oz court bouillon
$2\frac{1}{2}$ fl oz double cream
   (lightly whipped)
salt
paprika pepper

To finish
$2\frac{1}{4}$ fl oz thick mayonnaise
2-3 tablespoons tomato juice
sprigs of watercress (picked over)
head shell of lobster (split in two
   and lightly oiled)

*7-inch diameter top (No. 1 size)
soufflé dish, or cake tin*

Method
Lightly oil the dish or tin. Rinse
the lobster in cold water and
put into boiling court bouillon.
Cook for 30 minutes and leave to
cool in the liquid.

Prepare the velouté sauce and
leave to cool, covered with a
buttered greaseproof paper to
prevent a skin forming.

Shell the lobster, cut the tail
meat in slices, chop the claw
meat and scoop out all the soft
creamy meat from the head,
first removing the sac con-
taining weed. Oil and split the
head shell of the lobster, and set
aside. Shell the eggs, chop the
whites and sieve the yolks. Soak
the gelatine in the $2\frac{1}{2}$ fl oz court
bouillon, then dissolve it over
gentle heat.

Mix the velouté sauce, mayonnaise, egg yolks and whites, gelatine and the claw and soft creamy meat together, and season to taste. When the mixture begins to thicken, fold in the cream and pour mousse into the oiled dish or tin, leave it in a cool place to set.

For serving : turn out the mousse, coat with the mayonnaise, thinned with the tomato juice, and arrange the slices of tail on top. Garnish with the head shell and watercress.

Some of the raw ingredients for making a lobster mousse

Lobster Newburg

1½-2 lb lobster
court bouillon
about 1 oz butter
1 sherry glass brandy, or Madeira
salt and pepper
boiled rice (for serving)

For sauce
3 egg yolks
7½ fl oz double cream
1-1½ oz butter
salt and pepper
½ teaspoon paprika pepper —
    (optional)

Lobster Newburg is an exception to the rule that hot lobster dishes should be made from raw lobster. Here the lobster is previously boiled and the meat carefully warmed in the rich creamy sauce. Naturally the flavour is better if the lobster is freshly boiled at home, but if the time factor is important, buy a cooked lobster.

Method

Rinse live lobster and put into boiling court bouillon. Cook for about 30 minutes and cool in the liquid. Take up, snip down the soft shell under the tail with scissors. Peel off the hard shell, keeping the tail whole. Crack claws and extract meat. Rub a shallow stewpan or sauté pan well with butter. Put in claw meat and tail, cut in 'scallops'. Season, heat gently for 2-3 minutes. Then flame with the brandy or Madeira. Draw aside.

Beat egg yolks, add cream and the butter in tiny pieces. Season well and, if wished, flavour delicately with a little paprika fried first in ¼ oz of the sauce butter. Pour this sauce over the lobster, heat slowly, swirling the pan gently until the sauce is thick and creamy. Serve lobster at once with boiled rice.

If preferred, the egg liaison may be first lightly thickened over heat before pouring over the lobster meat.

To flame :

Dishes are flamed (flambé) with a spirit such as brandy or a fortified wine, eg. sherry. The spirit or wine must be heated in order to make the spirit more volatile, and so catch alight quickly. It is then poured, flaming, over the dish.

The food must be hot and sizzling, otherwise the flame will go out and the object of the flaming be lost. If correctly done, this process slightly singes the surface of the food, the alcohol is burnt away, and the juices that remain give colour and flavour to the sauce.

Flaming also burns up excess fat.

Devilled lobster

2 live lobsters (about ¾ lb each)
1½ oz butter
1 glass sherry
salt and pepper
3 fl oz double cream
watercress (to garnish)
6-8 oz rice (boiled)

For devil sauce
2 tablespoons Worcestershire
   sauce
2 tablespoons mushroom
   ketchup
1 teaspoon tomato purée
1 teaspoon tarragon vinegar
1 teaspoon chopped onion
1 clove of garlic (crushed with
   1 teaspoon salt)
2 slices of lemon (cut in half)
black pepper (ground from mill)
1 bayleaf
1 wineglass red wine (Bordeaux)
1 wineglass court bouillon
¼-½ lb tomatoes (skinned and
   shredded)

Method
Put all the sauce ingredients, ex-
cept tomatoes, into a pan, cover
and simmer for 10-15 minutes.
Set aside, remove lemon.

Kill the lobsters with a knife
(see page 111). Split them in
two and remove sac and intestine. Sauté, cut side down,
in butter for 5 minutes. Flame
with the sherry, add half a cup
of the devil sauce, cover and
cook on top or in oven at 350°F
or Mark 4 for 10-15 minutes.
Then take up, remove meat from
claws and tail, slice and replace.
Boil up rest of sauce, add tomatoes, adjust seasoning, add
cream.

Dish up the lobsters, pour
the sauce over, garnish with
watercress and serve at once
with boiled rice.

Lobster gratiné

2 live lobsters (about 1 lb each)
2 tablespoons oil
1 oz butter
2 shallots (finely chopped)
1½ wineglasses dry white wine
béchamel sauce (made with ¾ oz
   butter and ¾ oz flour, 7½ fl oz
   flavoured milk)
salt and pepper
2½ fl oz double cream

To finish
browned crumbs
grated Parmesan cheese
melted butter

Method
Kill lobsters with a knife (see
page 111). Split them, remove
sac from head and crack claws.
Put at once into hot oil and
butter, cover tightly and cook on
low heat for about 3-4 minutes.
Put the pan into the oven at
350°F or Mark 4 for 10-15 min-
nutes, then remove and cool
slightly.

Cook the shallots in the wine
until this is reduced by half, add
to the béchamel sauce with the
strained juice from the lobster.
Reboil, season and add cream.
Simmer until thick. Remove
lobster from shell, chop claw
meat and mix with 3-4 tablespoons of the sauce.

Slice tail meat into 'scallops',
pour a little of the sauce into
the halved shells, place the
claw meat in the head and
arrange the 'scallops' in the
tail. Coat the whole with the
remaining sauce and finish with
the crumbs, cheese and butter.
Brown in the oven at 400°F or
Mark 6 and serve very hot.

Omelet Barante

6-8 eggs
1 small freshly cooked lobster
    (poached in court bouillon)
6 oz firm white mushrooms
2-3 oz butter
salt and pepper
$2\frac{1}{2}$ fl oz port
1 small carton ($2\frac{1}{2}$ fl oz) double
    cream
$\frac{1}{2}$ pint light mornay sauce (made
    with milk flavoured as for
    béchamel sauce) — see page 12
3-4 tablespoons freshly grated
    Parmesan cheese

This delicious omelet was dedicated to the Baron de Barante, a famous 19th century gourmet and historian. It was also Edward VII's favourite omelet.

Method

Crack claws and remove shell from lobster. Cut the tail meat into scallops. Wipe the mushrooms, trim stalks level with the caps and slice evenly. Sauté these in half the butter for 4-5 minutes, then season lightly. Add port, cover and reduce to half quantity, draw aside and pour in the cream. Add the lobster meat, cover and simmer for 4-5 minutes, then draw aside.

Prepare the mornay sauce. Break the eggs into a bowl and beat to a light froth, add 2 tablespoons water and season. Make the omelet in the usual way, using the rest of the butter. While it is still soft and creamy in the middle spoon in the lobster mixture, then roll up and turn on to an ovenproof dish for serving. Coat at once with the sauce, sprinkle well with the freshly grated cheese and brown under the grill.

Spooning lobster and mushroom filling into the omelet Barante before rolling it up

Turning the finished omelet Barante on to a serving dish

Right : omelet Barante is shown with a garnish of small lobsters

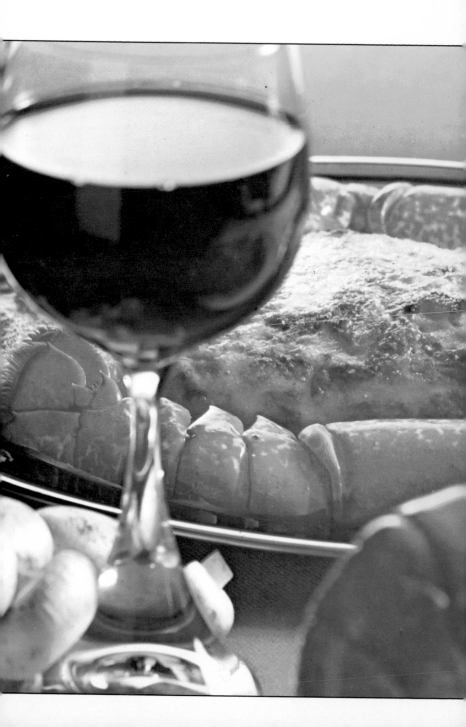

Spanish lobster

1-1½ lb lobster meat, or
   1 large can (12 oz) claw meat
2-3 tablespoons olive oil
2 onions (finely sliced)
1 glass sherry (optional)
3-4 ripe tomatoes (skinned ,
   quartered, seeds removed)
salt and pepper
1 wineglass stock
small bunch of chives
squeeze of lemon juice

*Spanish lobster can be prepared
at the table, in a chafing dish*

Method

Heat the oil in a pan, then add the onion. Lower the heat and stir occasionally until onion is tender and just turning colour. Then add the sherry (if using) and tomatoes. Season well and cook to a pulp. Put in the lobster, heat gently and add enough stock to moisten. There should be enough of this sauce to coat the lobster nicely. When hot, adjust the seasoning and snip in the chives. Add lemon juice and serve hot with buttered toast, or boiled rice.

Lobster pilaf

2 lobsters ($\frac{3}{4}$ lb each), or
  1 lobster (1$\frac{1}{2}$ lb)
2 pints court bouillon
$\frac{1}{2}$ pint béchamel sauce (made
  with 1 oz butter, 1 oz flour and
  $\frac{1}{2}$ pint flavoured milk)
1$\frac{1}{2}$ oz butter
paprika pepper
$\frac{1}{2}$ glass sherry
2 egg yolks
$\frac{1}{4}$ pint double cream

For pilaf
$\frac{1}{2}$ lb rice
1$\frac{1}{4}$ oz butter
1 oz onion (finely chopped)
1-1$\frac{1}{4}$ pints chicken, or veal,
  stock
salt and pepper
pinch of saffron (soaked in 2
  tablespoons boiling water for
  30 minutes)

Ring mould

Method
Rinse the lobster in cold water, put into boiling court bouillon and cook for 20-30 minutes, depending on the size. Meanwhile prepare the béchamel sauce and set the oven at 350°F or Mark 4.

To make the pilaf : melt two-thirds of the butter, add the onion and cook slowly until soft but not coloured. Add the rice and fry for a few minutes until it looks clear. Pour in 1 pint of the stock, season and add the saffron. Bring to the boil, cover and cook in the pre-set moderate oven until the rice is tender and all the stock absorbed, adding more stock as and when necessary. Fork in the remaining butter and fill the lightly oiled mould with rice.

To make the lobster salpicon : split the heads of the lobsters and scrape out the coral and the soft creamy meat. Mix this with 1 oz of the butter, rub through a fine strainer and keep on one side. Cut the flesh away from the tail shell and slice into scallops. Remove the meat from the claws.

Melt the remaining butter, add the paprika and cook very gently for about 1 minute. Then add the lobster meat and sherry and re-heat carefully. Mix the egg yolks and cream together. Add to the béchamel sauce and mix with the lobster. Stir carefully until the mixture thickens. Stir in the lobster butter in small pieces.

Turn the rice out of the mould on to a serving dish and fill the centre with the lobster salpicon. Garnish the dish with the lobster's head shell and feelers rubbed with a little oil.

Lobster thermidor

2 live lobsters (about ¾-1 lb each)
2 tablespoons oil
1½ oz butter
béchamel sauce (made with 1 oz
    butter, scant 1 oz flour, 7½ fl oz
    flavoured milk)
2 shallots (finely chopped)
1 wineglass dry white wine
1 teaspoon each tarragon and
    chervil (chopped), or pinch of
    dried herbs
2 tablespoons double cream
½ teaspoon French mustard
2 tablespoons grated Parmesan
    cheese
salt and pepper

To finish
browned crumbs
melted butter
watercress

Method

Kill lobsters (see page 111), split and remove sac and intestine. Have ready the oil and 1 oz of the butter, heated in a sauté pan. Put in the lobster, cut side downwards, cover· pan and cook gently for 12-15 minutes or until the lobster is red. Turn once only.

Make béchamel sauce and set aside in pan. Put shallot in a smaller saucepan with rest of butter, cook for ½ minute then add wine and herbs. Reduce to half quantity then add to the béchamel sauce. Set this mixture on low heat.

Take out the lobsters and strain any juice into the sauce. Stir well, add cream. Simmer for 2-3 minutes, then draw aside and mix in mustard and half the cheese. Season, cover pan and leave off heat.

Take out lobster meat, coarsely chopping claw meat and slicing tail into 'scallops'.

Add 1-2 tablespoons of sauce to the claw meat and put into the head shells. Put 1 tablespoon of sauce into the tail shells and replace 'scallops', rounded side up. Place shells on a baking sheet, wedging them with a piece of potato or on circles of claws. Coat lobster with rest of sauce, sprinkle with crumbs, rest of cheese and a little melted butter. Brown in the oven at 400°F or Mark 6 for 7-10 minutes. Garnish with watercress and serve very hot on a napkin.

Watchpoint This dish can be prepared in the morning and left ready for browning before serving in the evening.

Note : if there is coral (spawn) in the lobster, remove after splitting. Work on a plate with a palette knife, adding about ½ oz butter, then rub through a bowl strainer. Lobster thermidor does not have coral added but if you have no other immediate use for it (such as for a soup) add it to the sauce with the cream.

Coating the cooked lobsters

Lobster américaine

1 lobster (1½-2 lb)
1½ tablespoons salad oil
2½ tablespoons brandy
2 oz butter
1 small onion (finely chopped)
1 clove of garlic (finely chopped)
salt and pepper
¾ lb tomatoes (skinned, seeds
   removed, flesh chopped quite
   finely)
1 wineglass white wine
1 cup cooked vegetables
   (diced French beans, turnips and
   carrots in equal quantities)
¾ oz plain flour
1 teaspoon tomato purée
1 wineglass stock

Method

Kill the lobster (see page 111) and split the head in two. Cut the tail crossways into scallops. Remove the soft creamy parts and any coral from the head and keep on one side. Heat the oil, add the pieces of lobster tail and sauté gently, shell side downwards, until turning colour. Flame with the brandy (see page 114). Remove from the pan, add half the butter and the onion and garlic and cook slowly for 5 minutes, then add the seasoning, chopped tomato flesh and wine. Simmer for 10 minutes. Add the diced vegetables and a little stock if the tomatoes were not very juicy.

Work the remaining butter with the lobster coral, creamy meat from the head, flour and tomato purée and rub through a nylon strainer. Remove the pan from the heat, add this lobster butter a small piece at a time, blend, or shake in the pan to mix, and then reboil carefully. Cut the soft part of the lobster shell on the underside of each piece of tail meat (this enables the flesh to be removed easily when eating) and return tail meat to the pan. Reheat carefully, dish up and serve with plainly boiled rice.

Moules marinière

2 quarts mussels
1 onion (quartered)
1 carrot (quartered)
1 stick of celery (sliced)
large bouquet garni
1 wineglass white wine
(optional)
1 wineglass water, or 2 if no
wine is used
1 oz butter
1 rounded tablespoon plain flour
1 rounded tablespoon coarsely
chopped fresh parsley
pepper

Piece of butter muslin

Moules marinière are eaten
from soup plates and may be
dished up in these with the
sauce poured over them. Have
a large bowl in the middle of
the table for empty shells.

Method

Thoroughly scrub the mussels,
making sure that all are tightly
closed, and put into a large pan.
Tuck the vegetables down
among the mussels with the
bouquet garni. Pour over the
liquid, cover pan with a close-
fitting lid and put on moderate
heat. Leave until the liquid boils
right up over mussels. Draw pan
aside at once.

Work the butter and flour
together and set aside. Strain
mussel liquid from pan through
a piece of butter muslin into a
smaller pan. Then add the
kneaded butter, piece by piece,
off the heat, whisking it in well.
Put this pan on heat, bring to
the boil and cook gently for 4-5
minutes. Add the parsley and
season well with pepper.

Turn the mussels into a deep
dish and pour over the sauce.

*Moules marinière are best eaten with a fork and your fingers ; as this
dish is quite messy, put out finger bowls and a spoon for the juice. Open
mussels with your fingers, and prise flesh from shells with a fork*

Mussel soup

1 quart mussels
1 lb sole bones
1 onion (sliced and blanched)
6 white peppercorns
1½ oz butter
bouquet garni
juice of ½ lemon
salt
2 wineglasses white wine
1 clove of garlic
1¼ pints stock, or water
½ oz plain flour
2 egg yolks
2½ fl oz double cream
1 dessertspoon chopped parsley

Put the well-washed fish bones in a saucepan with onion, peppercorns, ½ oz of butter, bouquet garni and lemon juice. Cover the pan and cook over very gentle heat for 10 minutes. Add salt, 1 glass of wine, garlic and stock or water and simmer for 20 minutes.

Melt the remaining butter in a pan, stir in the flour and cook gently until straw-coloured, then strain fish stock on to this and bring to the boil. Simmer for 15 minutes.

Meanwhile, wash and scrub the mussels, put into a pan with the rest of the wine. Bring to the boil, then strain the liquor into the soup.

Shell the mussels and discard the beards, add the mussels to the soup and simmer for 5 minutes. Mix the egg yolks with cream and add this liaison to the soup. Reheat without boiling, add the parsley and serve.

The cleaned mussels ready for cooking in wine to make mussel soup

Mussels with rice

2 quarts mussels
1 onion (sliced)
1 carrot (sliced)
bouquet garni
6 peppercorns
1 wineglass white wine
1 wineglass water
1 lb tomatoes
black pepper (ground from mill)

For pilaf
3 oz butter
1 onion (chopped)
2 sticks of celery (sliced)
6 oz rice
about 1 pint water, or light
  chicken stock
pinch of saffron (soaked in 1
  egg cup of boiling water), or
  little mussel liquor

Muslin (fine or butter)

Method

Throughly wash and scrub the mussels, making sure that they are all tightly closed, and put into a large pan with vegetables, bouquet garni and peppercorns. Pour over the wine and water, cover the pan and shake over moderate heat until the liquid boils up and over the mussels. Cook a few minutes until the mussels open. Set pan aside.

Scald and skin the tomatoes, cut in quarters, remove the seeds and the small hard core.

Remove the mussels from their shells with a sharp knife, pull away the beards and strain the liquid through fine muslin, then reserve it. Mix mussels with the tomatoes and keep on one side.

To prepare the pilaf : melt half the butter, add the onion and celery and cook for 2-3 minutes until the onion is soft but not coloured ; add the rice and stir over heat for a further 2-3 minutes.

Pour on the water or stock, add saffron or a little of the mussel liquor. Bring to the boil, cover the pan (or transfer to a covered casserole) and cook in a moderate oven at 375°F or Mark 5 for 20-30 minutes or until the rice is tender.

Fork the mussels and tomatoes carefully into the rice with plenty of black pepper. Dot the remaining butter on the top and, if the rice is dry, add about another tablespoon of the mussel liquor. Leave to stand about 10 minutes before serving.

Mussel chowder

1 can mussels (14 oz)
4 oz green streaky bacon
1 large onion (chopped)
1 stick of celery (chopped)
1 green pepper (blanched and chopped)
2 medium-size potatoes (diced)
1 small bayleaf
$\frac{3}{4}$ pint water
salt and pepper
1$\frac{1}{4}$ oz plain flour
1 pint milk
1 dessertspoon chopped parsley

Method

Remove the rind and cut bacon into dice ; sizzle gently in a dry pan until turning colour, then add the onion and celery and cook until golden-brown. Add the green pepper, potatoes, bayleaf and water and bring to the boil. Season, and simmer until potatoes are tender, then draw pan aside.

Blend the flour with $\frac{1}{2}$ cup of the milk and add to the chowder ; stir until boiling. Heat the rest of the milk and add to the chowder with the drained mussels ; simmer 4-5 minutes before turning into a soup tureen. Scatter parsley over top.

Chowder, an American speciality, is a soup stew made from shellfish (or white fish) with vegetables and unsmoked bacon or salt pork, according to the recipe.

It was introduced to the United States by early French settlers, and the word originates either from 'chaudrée de Fouras', a fish soup from the Fouras region of France, or from 'chaudière' (kettle).

Mussels, bacon and vegetables make a delicious thick soup

Mussel salad

2 quarts mussels
1 onion (sliced)
1 carrot (sliced)
1 wineglass white wine
$\frac{1}{4}$ pint water
bouquet garni
6-8 peppercorns
$\frac{1}{4}$ pint chicken stock
4 oz rice
3 tablespoons oil
1 shallot (finely chopped)
$\frac{1}{2}$ bayleaf
1 head of celery
4 oz white mushrooms
juice of $\frac{1}{2}$ lemon
pepper (ground from mill)
4 tablespoons double cream
1 tablespoon chopped parsley

Method

Wash and scrub the mussels, making sure they are all tightly closed, and place in a saucepan with the onion, carrot, wine, water, bouquet garni and peppercorns. Cover the pan and bring to the boil. Now shake the pan once or twice and simmer for 2-3 minutes, until all the mussel shells are open. Lift the mussels from the saucepan into a china bowl with a draining spoon and strain the liquid in the pan through muslin into another basin, measure and make up to $\frac{1}{2}$pint with chicken stock.

Wash the rice and put in a pan with the oil and the shallot. Pour over the mussel liquor (mixed with stock) and bring to the boil, add the bayleaf, cover the pan and cook until the rice is tender and the stock absorbed (about 18 minutes).

Meanwhile wash the celery and cut into batons about 1 inch long. Wash and trim the mushrooms, cut them in thick slices and leave marinating in the lemon juice and pepper.

Take the mussels from their shells and remove the beards. Mix the mussels with the mushrooms and turn the rice into a bowl to cool. Drain and dry the celery. When the rice is quite cold, mix the celery, mussels and mushrooms into it with a fork, taste for seasoning and then add the cream. Pile into an entrée dish and dust with chopped parsley.

Mussels, mushrooms and rice are the main ingredients for a good party salad

Oyster soup

12 oysters, or 1 can of oysters
2 oz butter
2 shallots (finely chopped)
$\frac{1}{2}$ teaspoon paprika pepper
pinch of ground mace
1 tablespoon cornflour
1 can (about 12 oz) evaporated
  milk
$\frac{3}{4}$ pint milk
salt and pepper

Method
Melt the butter and add the shallots, cover and cook slowly until golden. Add the paprika and mace, cook for 1 minute then blend in the cornflour, evaporated milk and milk. Season and stir until boiling, then simmer for 3-4 minutes. Remove the oysters from their shells, and add them, with any liquid (or canned ones with their juice), to the pan. Reheat carefully without boiling.

Angels on horseback

8 oysters (2 per person)
8 bacon rashers
4 slices of toast
butter (for toast)

Method
Wrap oysters in bacon rashers, fasten each roll with fine skewers and grill for 4-5 minutes, or bake in the oven for 5-6 minutes at 400°F or Mark 6.
  Serve on hot buttered toast.

Angels on horseback, served garnished with watercress

Prawns Alabama

4-6 Dublin Bay prawns per person,
 or 10 oz frozen prawns
lemon juice
black pepper (ground from mill)
lettuce leaves
paprika pepper

For Alabama sauce
4 fl oz tomato sauce, or tomato
 ketchup, or tomato juice
$\frac{1}{2}$ pint very thick mayonnaise
1 small head of celery (chopped),
 or $\frac{1}{2}$ cucumber (finely diced)
1 small, or $\frac{1}{2}$ large, green pepper
 (seeds removed and flesh
 chopped)
1 rounded tablespoon freshly grated
 horseradish
1 clove of garlic (crushed with $\frac{1}{4}$
 teaspoon salt)
2-3 tablespoons double cream
few drops of Tabasco sauce

This Alabama sauce can also
be used as a dip for a cocktail
party.

Method
Shell the Dublin Bay prawns, or
thaw out frozen prawns. Sprinkle
over a little lemon juice and
black pepper, then cover and
leave to marinate while preparing the sauce.

Add tomato sauce (or ketchup,
or juice) to mayonnaise, whisking
it well. If using cucumber,
sprinkle with salt and leave for
about 15 minutes, then drain
thoroughly. Add it, or celery, to
sauce, with chopped pepper,
horseradish, garlic, double
cream and Tabasco. The sauce
must be quite spicy and piquant
— add more seasoning if necessary.

Arrange the drained prawns
on the lettuce leaves on individual plates and coat with 2-3
tablespoons of sauce. Dust with
paprika and serve chilled. If
you wish, shred the lettuce and
put in coupe glasses with the
prawns and sauce on top.

Prawn cocktail

8 oz frozen prawns (allow at
  least 1½ oz per person)
1 small lettuce (finely shredded)
paprika pepper (for dusting)
4-8 prawns in their shells (for
  garnish)

For sauce
½ pint thick mayonnaise
1 dessertspoon tomato ketchup
salt and pepper
dash of Tabasco sauce
1 large tablespoon double cream
squeeze of lemon juice

Glass goblets for serving

Method
Thaw out prawns thoroughly.
Combine the sauce ingredients.
Add about half to the prawns,
just enough to coat nicely. Put
shredded lettuce in the bottom
of the goblets, arrange prawns
on top and coat with rest of
sauce. Dust with paprika and
garnish each serving with 1-2
fresh prawns, with the body and
tail shell removed but the head
left on.

Creamed prawns

½ lb prawns (shelled)
1½ oz butter
1 shallot (finely chopped)
1 teaspoon curry powder
salt and pepper
1 tablespoon plain flour
7-10 fl oz milk
1 cup frozen peas (thawed)

If using frozen prawns, thaw
out overnight in the refrigerator.

Method
Heat a pan, put in the butter,
add the shallot, curry powder
and seasoning. Simmer for
2-3 minutes, then stir in the
flour and add the milk. Stir until
boiling. Put in the peas and
simmer for 3-4 minutes. Then
add the prawns ; lower the heat
and leave until thoroughly hot.
Serve on toast as a first course.

Prawn chop suey

6-8 oz prawns (shelled)
4 tablespoons oil
1 large onion (sliced)
1 sweet pepper (core and seeds
    removed, flesh shredded)
1 large carrot (shredded)
2 sticks of celery (sliced)
1 can (8 oz) bean sprouts

For topping
1 large egg
1 tablespoon oil
salt and pepper

Method
Heat 3 tablespoons of oil in a
large frying pan and add the
onion, pepper, carrot and
celery. Shake the pan over
moderate heat until the vegetables are barely cooked, then
add prawns and the drained
bean sprouts, forking them in
well. Turn mixture into a round
dish for serving.

Wipe out pan, reheat with
remaining tablespoon of oil.
To prepare topping : beat egg
with oil, season and pour into
the pan. Cook gently until
egg is set, turn it with a slice
and cook for a further $\frac{1}{2}$
minute. Slide topping out on to
prawn chop suey and serve hot.

Sweet and sour prawns

16 Pacific prawns, or 1 lb small
    prawns
oil
chopped garlic
chilli sauce (to taste)
tomato ketchup (to taste)
1 dessertspoon cornflour (slaked
    with 2 tablespoon water)
8 oz fried rice
1 cup canned bean sprouts

Method
Allow prawns to thaw out
completely, then drain well.

Heat oil in a deep frying pan,
add prawns and fry briskly for
5-6 minutes, turning them frequently. Add the garlic and,
after a few minutes, the chilli
sauce and tomato ketchup.
Heat thoroughly and bind with
the cornflour.

Continue to cook 2-3 min-
utes, then serve with fried
rice into which the drained bean
sprouts have been stirred.

Timbale à l'indienne

8 oz quantity of rich shortcrust pastry
paprika pepper

For curry sauce
2 small onions
1 oz butter
1 dessertspoon curry powder
béchamel sauce (made with 1 oz
   butter, 1 oz plain flour, $\frac{3}{4}$ pint
   flavoured milk)
1-2 tablespoons double cream
salt and pepper (optional)

For filling
6 oz prawns (shelled)
3 hard-boiled eggs (quartered)
3 oz long grain rice (boiled)

Deep 7-8 inch diameter sandwich tin

Method
Line pastry into the sandwich tin and bake blind.

To prepare curry sauce : chop onions very finely, cook them in butter until soft but not coloured, then add curry powder and cook for 3-4 minutes. Add the béchamel sauce and simmer for 2-3 minutes, then add the cream and seasoning, if necessary.

Fill pastry case with alternate layers of prawns, eggs and rice, and the sauce, piling up the mixture well and finishing with prawns. Dust the top with paprika pepper and hand any remaining sauce separately.

Timbale à l'indienne, a prawn flan with curry sauce

Prawn gougère

For choux pastry
$\frac{1}{4}$ pint water
2 oz butter
2$\frac{1}{2}$ oz plain flour (sifted)
2 eggs (beaten)
2 oz Cheddar cheese (diced)
salt and pepper

For filling
8 oz prawns (shelled)
1 medium-size onion
$\frac{1}{2}$ oz butter
1 dessertspoon plain flour
$\frac{1}{2}$ pint stock, or milk
1 teaspoon chopped parsley
2 tomatoes (skinned, seeds
  removed, and shredded)
1 tablespoon finely grated
  Parmesan cheese
1 tablespoon browned breadcrumbs
chopped parsley (to garnish)

*Deep 8-inch diameter pie plate, or
ovenproof dish, or 6 small individual cocottes*

Gougère is a savoury choux
pastry dish mixed with cheese
and served plain, or with a
savoury filling.

Method
Prepare the choux pastry by
bringing $\frac{1}{4}$ pint water and the
butter to the boil, draw pan
aside, add the sifted flour all
at once, then stir vigorously
until paste is smooth. Cool,
then add the eggs, a little
at a time, beating them in
thoroughly. Stir in the cheese
and season.

Set oven at 400°F or Mark 6.

To prepare filling : slice the
onion and cook it slowly in the
butter until soft. Draw the pan
aside, stir in the flour and pour
in the stock (or milk), stir until
boiling.

Take pan off the heat and
add the prawns, parsley and
shredded tomatoes. Well
butter the pie plate (or ovenproof dish or cocottes), arrange
the choux pastry around the
sides, hollowing out the centre.
Pour the filling into this, dust
with grated cheese and crumbs
mixed together. Bake in pre-set
oven for 30-40 minutes (or 15-20
minutes for individual cocottes).
When choux is well risen and
evenly browned, take gougère
out of oven and sprinkle well with
the chopped parsley before serving.

Prawns in aspic

4-6 oz prawns (shelled)
$1\frac{1}{2}$ pints aspic jelly made with
  fish stock — (see page 58)

For garnish
pimiento
chervil
1 box of small cress
8 prawns

8 dariole, or castle, moulds

Method

Line the moulds with a thin coating of cool aspic jelly, making a layer of about $\frac{1}{4}$ inch on the bottom of each one. Cut a small round of pimiento for each mould, dip this into a little aspic jelly and place it at the bottom of each one. Put a small sprig of chervil at each side of the pimiento rounds. Cool 1 tablespoon aspic jelly at a time on a cube of ice and run this on to the decoration to hold it in position. Leave to set.

Arrange prawns and remaining aspic jelly in layers until the moulds are full, finishing with aspic. Pour any aspic left over into a shallow tin to use for decoration ; leave in a cool place to set, then chop it roughly.

Allow at least 1-2 hours before turning out prawns. If serving them on a silver or steel dish, run a thin coating of cool aspic over the bottom of the dish and leave it to set. Unmould the prawns carefully by dipping them in hot water and serve them on the dish, garnished with small cress, chopped aspic and the few reserved prawns ; serve them with brown bread and butter.

1 Using a skewer to arrange the pimiento and chervil in moulds
2 Layering prawns and aspic in moulds ; stand them in a tray of ice to quicken the setting

Careful decoration and a silver serving dish for prawn and aspic moulds

Eggs mimosa

4 **large eggs (hard-boiled)**
4-6 oz shrimps, or prawns
   (shelled and coarsely chopped)
$\frac{1}{2}$ **pint thick mayonnaise**
watercress (to garnish)

One of the best and simplest egg dishes for a first course. Serve with brown bread and butter.

Method

Cool eggs and peel. Split them in half lengthways, scoop out yolks and carefully push half of them through a bowl strainer into a basin. Add the shrimps or prawns. Mix and bind with 1-2 tablespoons mayonnaise.

Wash whites, dry and set on a serving dish. Fill with the prawn mixture. Thin the rest of the mayonnaise slightly with 1 tablespoon hot water and coat the eggs with this.

Hold strainer over eggs and push rest of the yolks through. Garnish dish with watercress.

1 *Sieving half the egg yolks*
2 *Mixing sieved yolks with prawns and thick mayonnaise*
3 *The remaining yolks are sieved over the eggs mimosa to garnish*

Curried Pacific prawns

6-8 Pacific prawns (frozen,
    fresh, or canned)
court bouillon (for poaching
    fresh prawns)
1 tablespoon milk, and pepper
    (for frozen, or canned, prawns)

For curry cream sauce
1 medium-size onion (chopped)
1 oz butter
1 teaspoon curry paste
1 dessertspoon curry powder
1 dessertspoon plain flour
1 teaspoon tomato purée
scant $\frac{1}{2}$ pint light veal stock
1 dessertspoon redcurrant jelly
$2\frac{1}{2}$ fl oz coconut milk
juice of $\frac{1}{2}$ lemon
$2\frac{1}{2}$ fl oz double cream

For accompaniments
boiled rice
fresh coconut (put through a
    nutmill)
4 oz currants (soaked overnight,
    brought slowly to the boil,
    simmered for 3-4 minutes)
crushed pineapple (mixed with
    sliced crystallised ginger)

Method

First prepare the curry sauce.
Chop the onion and cook it for
3-4 minutes in the butter, then
add the curry paste and powder
and continue to cook for 3-4
minutes. Then stir in the flour,
tomato purée and stock. Bring
to the boil, cover and simmer
for 8-15 minutes. Draw aside,
add the redcurrant jelly, coconut milk and lemon juice and
cook for a further 7 minutes.

If the prawns are fresh (uncooked), poach them in a little
court bouillon for about 7
minutes. If they are canned or
frozen, turn them out into a pan
with about 1 tablespoon of milk
and a little pepper and re-heat
carefully.

Draw the sauce aside and add
the cream. Turn it into a serving
dish and arrange the prawns on
top. Serve hot with the accompaniments ; the rice in a large
dish and the three other accompaniments in small bowls.

*Pacific prawns are a luxury served
in a good curry sauce*

Tomato chartreuse with prawns

For chartreuse
$\frac{3}{4}$ pint tomato juice, or 1 pint
   canned tomatoes
strip of lemon rind
$\frac{1}{2}$-1 teaspoon tomato purée
3-4 peppercorns
1 bayleaf
1 clove of garlic (well bruised)
salt
sugar (to taste)
pepper (freshly ground from
   mill)
$\frac{1}{2}$ oz gelatine (softened in 2-3
   tablespoons cold water)
lemon juice (to taste)

For dressing
2 tablespoons wine vinegar
6 tablespoons olive oil
salt, pepper and mustard (to
   taste)
1$\frac{1}{4}$ oz walnuts (ground through
   nut mill)
6 oz prawns, or shrimps (shelled)

To garnish
watercress

Ring mould (2$\frac{1}{2}$ pints capacity)

Method
First prepare the chartreuse.
Put the tomato juice or canned
tomatoes into a pan with the
lemon rind, tomato purée,
peppercorns, bayleaf, garlic,
salt, sugar and pepper to taste.
Bring slowly to the boil. Simmer
gently for 5 minutes. Strain
the juice or press the pulp
through a strainer into a
measure. If it does not make
$\frac{3}{4}$ pint, make it up to this
amount with water. Now stir
in the softened gelatine, adjust
the seasoning and add lemon
juice. Cool, pour into a wet ring
mould and leave to set.

Combine the vinegar, oil and
seasonings for the dressing.
Then add the ground walnuts
and the picked (ie. shelled)
prawns, or shrimps. Turn out
the chartreuse, arrange the
watercress in the centre and
serve the prawn/shrimp and
walnut dressing separately.

Scampi gourmet

1 lb scampi
1 oz butter (melted)
salt and pepper
dash of Tabasco sauce

For white wine sauce
1 shallot (finely chopped)
1 wineglass white wine
2 egg yolks
1 oz butter
2½ fl oz double cream
lemon juice
7½ fl oz velouté sauce (made
 with ¾ oz butter, ½ oz flour and
 7½ fl oz fish stock) — see method,
 page 19

For garnish
2-3 tomatoes (scalded, skinned,
 quartered, seeds removed)
12 fresh, or 1 small can,
 asparagus tips
2 oz button mushrooms (sliced)
1 oz butter

Method

First prepare the sauce : simmer shallot in the wine until the liquid is reduced by half. Work the egg yolks well with half of the butter, then strain on the reduced wine. Thicken over gentle heat, then add the rest of the butter a little at a time. Finish with the cream and lemon juice. Add the velouté sauce and gently heat without boiling, then set aside to keep warm.

Now prepare the garnish. Melt the butter and quickly sauté the quartered tomatoes, asparagus tips and sliced mushrooms.

Poach the scampi for 6-7 minutes (in the melted butter with the seasoning) in a covered pot on top of the stove or in the oven. Arrange them in a gratin dish, spoon the garnish on the top and coat with the sauce. Glaze lightly under the grill before serving.

Couronne of shrimps in aspic

6 oz shrimps, or prawns (shelled)
4 tomatoes
1 head of celery, or 1 bunch of
    watercress
$\frac{1}{2}$ pint mayonnaise
1$\frac{1}{2}$ pints aspic jelly

*Ring, or border, mould (1$\frac{1}{2}$-1$\frac{3}{4}$ pints
    capacity)*

Method

Scald and skin the tomatoes, cut them in four, scoop out the seeds into a small strainer and reserve the juice. Line the mould with a little cool aspic, arrange the quarters of tomato on this, rounded side down, and with the points towards the outer rim of the mould. Spoon over enough cold but still liquid aspic to hold the tomatoes in position and leave to set. Fill the mould alternately with shrimps (or prawns) and cool aspic, and leave to set.

Cut the celery into 2-inch lengths, then shred them into julienne strips. Leave these to soak and curl up in ice-cold water for about 30 minutes, then drain thoroughly.

To turn out the mould dip it into warm water, put your serving plate or dish over it, quickly turn it over ; the jelly should slide out easily. Fill the centre with the celery curls (or washed sprigs of watercress). Mix the mayonnaise with the juice strained from the tomato seeds and serve this separately with brown bread and butter.

Placing shrimps on tomatoes, before layering the remainder with aspic

Scallops with red wine and mushrooms

4 large scallops
¼ pint water
2-3 drops of lemon juice
1 oz butter
1 medium-size onion (finely chopped)
3 oz button mushrooms (quartered)
1 clove of garlic (crushed with salt)
1 rounded dessertspoon plain flour
1 wineglass of fish, or vegetable, stock, or liquor from scallops
1 teaspoon tomato purée
salt
black pepper (ground from mill)
1 wineglass red wine
2 tomatoes
4 tablespoons breadcrumbs (browned)
2 oz butter (melted)
creamed potatoes (for piping) — optional
parsley (chopped)

Scallops

The easiest way to open live scallops is to put the shells into a hot oven for 4-5 minutes. The heat will cause the shells to gape. Then carefully scrape away the fringe or beard which surrounds the scallop, and the black thread (intestine) which lies round it. Slip a sharp knife under the scallop to detach it and the roe from the shell.

Method

Remove scallops from shells, wash and dry shells well.

Put scallops into a shallow pan, pour on the water and add lemon juice. Cover and poach for 5 minutes. Turn into a basin, reserving liquid. Melt butter in the pan, add onion, cover and cook gently for 2 minutes. Put in mushrooms, increase heat and cook briskly for a further 2 minutes, stirring all the time. Draw pan aside, stir in garlic and flour and blend ; add the stock or liquor from the scallops, tomato purée and seasoning. Bring to the boil and simmer for 2-3 minutes.

Boil wine in a small pan until reduced by about a third. Add to the sauce and simmer for a further 5 minutes.

Scald and skin tomatoes, quarter and remove the seeds and cut away the little piece of hard stalk. Cut each piece of tomato in half lengthways and add to the sauce with the scallops. Spoon at once into the deep shells. Sprinkle well with the breadcrumbs tossed in melted butter.

If using creamed potato, pipe it round the shells to make a thick border before setting them on a baking sheet.

Put scallops in oven for about 5 minutes at 375°F or Mark 5 until they are brown. Dust with chopped parsley before serving.

Scallops pampolaise

8 scallops
1 wineglass white wine
1 wineglass water
$\frac{1}{2}$ bayleaf
6 peppercorns

For duxelles mixture
8 oz flat mushrooms
1 oz butter
2-3 shallots (finely chopped)
1 tablespoon chopped herbs
   (thyme, or marjoram, and
   parsley mixed)
salt and pepper

For velouté sauce
1 oz butter
1 scant oz plain flour
liquid in which the scallops
   were cooked
5 tablespoons top of the milk
1-2 tablespoons double cream
$1\frac{1}{2}$ oz grated cheese

4 large scallop shells

Method

Remove scallops from shells ;
wash and dry shells well.

Poach the scallops in wine
and water for 5 minutes, with the
bayleaf and peppercorns. Wash
and trim the mushrooms, chop
them finely and cook with the
shallots in the butter in a sauté
pan until much of the moisture
has been driven off. Add herbs
and season. Divide this duxelles
mixture among the shells.

Drain and halve the scallops.
Arrange on the top of the mushroom mixture ; keep warm.
Prepare the sauce in the usual
way, finishing with 1 oz of the
cheese. Coat the scallops with
sauce, sprinkle the rest of the
cheese over them and brown in
a quick oven or under the grill.

Scallops Cordon Bleu

6 scallops
$\frac{1}{4}$ pint hot water
squeeze of lemon juice
6 peppercorns
$\frac{1}{2}$ bayleaf
paprika pepper

For sauce
5 tablespoons boiling water
1 tablespoon ground almonds
$\frac{3}{4}$ oz butter
1 small onion (finely chopped)
1 teaspoon curry powder
1 tablespoon plain flour
1 teaspoon tomato purée
$\frac{1}{4}$ pint milk
juice of $\frac{1}{2}$ lemon
2 tablespoons double cream

Method

Remove scallops from shells ;
wash and dry shells well. Put
the scallops into a pan with
the water, lemon juice, peppercorns and bayleaf, bring to the
boil, poach gently for 6-7 minutes and leave in liquid.

To make sauce : pour boiling
water on to almonds, leave 10-15
minutes, then strain almond
'milk' through muslin into a
bowl.

Melt butter in a pan, add
onion and cook until soft but
not coloured, then add curry
powder and flour. Fry gently for
2 minutes, add tomato purée
and milk. Stir until boiling and
then simmer for 5 minutes, add
almond 'milk', sharpen with
lemon juice and then add the
cream. Drain scallops, cut in
four and add to sauce.

Serve scallops in the deep
shells, with boiled rice dusted
with paprika pepper down one
side.

Scallops parisienne

4 scallops
$\frac{1}{2}$ wineglass white wine
1 wineglass water
6 peppercorns
2-3 parsley stalks
$\frac{1}{2}$ bayleaf
3-4 jerusalem artichokes
    (depending on size)
little milk and water mixed (to
    cover artichokes)

For sauce
1 oz butter
1 small onion (finely chopped)
4 oz button mushrooms
    (quartered)
1 rounded tablespoon plain flour
stock (from scallops)
$\frac{1}{2}$ gill creamy milk
salt and pepper
4 tablespoons browned crumbs
2 oz butter (melted)
creamed potatoes (for piping) —
    optional

Scallops parisienne have
a mushroom sauce. Cor-
rectly, these should be the
small hard white buttons
known as champignons de
Paris, and if these are used
they should be left whole.
We have included arti-
chokes in this dish because
they have a delicate nutty
flavour which marries well
with the scallops, and they
make the dish go further.

Method

Take scallops out of shells and
wash and dry the shells. Put
scallops into a pan, pour in
wine and water, add peppercorns and herbs. Cover and
simmer for 5-6 minutes.

Peel and cut artichokes into
walnut-size pieces, simmer for
10 minutes or until just tender
in a little milk and water. Drain
and set aside.

To prepare sauce : melt butter,
add onion, cover and cook for
1 minute. Then add mushrooms,
cook briskly for 3-4 minutes.
Draw aside, stir in flour, strain
on the stock from the scallops
(which should measure $1\frac{1}{2}$ gills)
blend and stir until boiling, then
stir in the milk and seasoning.
Add the scallops, quartered, and
the artichokes. Mix carefully
and put into the shells, sprinkle
with crumbs and cover with
melted butter.

Pipe round the shells with
creamed potato, if wished, before putting in the oven at
350°F or Mark 4 for about 5-7
minutes, or until brown.

Appendix

Notes and basic recipes

To clean round fish

Rinse in cold water, then scrape with the back of a knife from tail to head to remove scales ; this applies particularly to scaly fish, such as herrings and salmon.

For large round fish, such as haddock, codling, sea trout, take a sharp knife and slit the skin from just below head, along belly to the vent. Scrape out the gut, discard ; the head may then be cut off. Hold fish under a running cold tap to clean it thoroughly. If there is any black skin inside the cavity (sometimes there is, even though the fish has been bought gutted), gently rub it away with a damp cloth dipped in salt.

To clean flat fish

With fish such as plaice or sole, make a semi-circular cut just below head on the dark side, scrape out the gut and wash fish thoroughly.

To skin fillets of round fish

Lay skin side down on the board, lift the tail end and slip a thin, sharp knife in between the flesh and skin. Dip the fingers of your left hand in salt to prevent slipping and, holding the tail skin firmly, saw the flesh away from the skin, keeping the knife at an angle to the board.

To skin flat fish

Sole may be skinned whole and the fishmonger will skin them on both sides if asked.

When doing it yourself, trim away the outside fins with scissors. Lay the fish on the board and, starting at the head end, slip your thumb about 1 inch under the black skin at the cut where the fish was cleaned. Run your thumb right round the fish, then grasp the tail end of the skin firmly and rip it off. Repeat this on the other side of the fish.

Plaice are skinned after filleting, as the skin is thick and would tear the flesh if ripped off. Skin as for fillets of round fish.

To fillet round fish

Lay the fish on a piece of wet, rough cloth, or sacking (to prevent slipping) and keep fish steady with one hand. Take a thin sharp knife or filleting knife, and first trim away the fins then cut down the back with the blade on top of the backbone. Lift off the top fillet. Now slip the knife under the bone at the head, and keeping it as close as possible to the back bone, work down to the tail, using short sharp strokes, at the same time keeping a firm hold on the head with the other hand.

To fillet flat fish

Plaice and sole (if weighing no more than 1-1½ lb) are usually cut into a double fillet. This means that the flesh on both sides of the backbone, top and underside, is taken off in one piece, ie. two fillets only for each fish. These may be divided into two for cooking. Lemon sole is treated in the same way.

If filleting at home, it is easier to take the flesh off in four fillets. Run the point of the knife down the backbone and with short, sharp strokes keeping the knife on the bone, work from the head outwards until the tail is reached and the fillet is detached. Turn the fish round and starting from the tail take the other half of the fillet off in the same way. Then turn the fish over and repeat the process. Flat fish fillets are larger and thicker on the dark side, which is upper-most when the fish is swimming.

Deep fat frying

Choose a deep heavy gauge pan (fat bath or deep fryer) which covers source of heat, complete with a wire basket to fit. Or buy a separate folding wire basket for fitting into any saucepan (which must, however, be of reasonably heavy gauge because fat is heated to high temperatures in deep fat frying). This separate basket is useful when only occasionally deep fat frying because its flexibility means it can be used in an ordinary frying pan for cooking small foods such as croûtons.

When frying foods coated in soft batter mixture, you may find it easier to fry them in a fat bath without using a wire basket since batter tends to stick to the basket.

Suitable fats to use are : vegetable or nut oil ; lard ; clarified dripping or commercially prepared fat, but it is better not to mix these. Olive oil and margarine are not suitable for deep frying. Never fill pan with more than one-third fat or oil.

Melt the fat, or put the oil, over moderate heat, then increase heat until right cooking temperature is reached (for tests, see below). Oil must never be heated above 375°F, and for sunflower oil, and some commercially prepared fats (eg. Spry, Cookeen), 360°F is the highest recommended temperature. It is important to remember that oil does not 'haze', as solid fats do, until heated to a much higher temperature than is required — or is safe — for frying.

Apart from food cooked on a rising temperature (eg. pirozhki), the fat or oil should never be below 340°F, as it is essential that the surface of the food is sealed immediately. This means that it does not absorb the fat, and is more digestible.

The best way of testing temperature is with a frying thermometer. Before using, it should be stood in a pan of hot water then carefully dried before putting into the fat bath. The hot water warms the glass so that it does not break when plunged into the hot fat.

If you have no thermometer, drop in a small piece of the food to be cooked (eg. a chip). If the fat or oil is at the right temperature, the food will rise immediately to the top and bubbles appear round it. Alternatively drop in a cube of day-old bread, which should turn golden-brown in 20 seconds at 375°F ; 60 seconds at 360°F.

Béchamel sauce

$\frac{1}{2}$ **pint milk**
1 slice of onion
1 small bayleaf
6 peppercorns
1 blade mace
$\frac{3}{4}$ **oz butter**
$\frac{1}{2}$ **oz plain flour**
salt and pepper

Method
Put onion and spices in the milk and heat gently, without boiling, in a covered saucepan for 5-7 minutes.

Pour off into a jug and wipe out the pan. Melt the butter in this, and stir in the flour off the heat. Strain in a good third of the milk, blend and add remaining milk. When thoroughly mixed, season lightly, return to the heat and stir continually until boiling. Boil for 2-3 minutes, then adjust the seasoning.

Breadcrumbs

To make crumbs : take a large loaf (the best type to use is a sandwich loaf) at least two days old. Cut off the crust and keep to one side. Break up bread into crumbs either by rubbing through a wire sieve or a Mouli sieve, or by working in an electric blender.

To make dried crumbs : spread crumbs on a sheet of paper laid on a baking tin and cover with another sheet of paper to keep off any dust. Leave to dry in a warm temperature — the plate rack, or warming drawer, or the top of the oven, or even the airing cupboard, is ideal. The crumbs may take a day or two to dry thoroughly, and they must be crisp before storing in a jar. To make them uniformly fine, sift them through a wire bowl strainer.

To make browned crumbs : bake the crusts in a slow oven until golden-brown, then crush or grind through a mincer. Sift and store as for dried white crumbs. These browned ones are known as raspings and are used for any dish that is coated with a sauce and browned in the oven.

'Fish' potatoes

These are shaped from old potatoes and get their name because they so frequently accompany fish dishes.

Choose medium-size potatoes, peel and quarter them lengthways. Pare away sharp edges with a peeler and shape into ovals. Boil in a pan of salted water about 7 minutes, drain and return to pan. Cover with some foil or muslin and the pan lid. Complete cooking on a low heat until tender (about 4-5 minutes).

This treatment prevents potatoes from breaking and makes them dry and floury.

French dressing

Mix 1 tablespoon wine, or tarragon, vinegar with $\frac{1}{2}$ teaspoon each of salt and freshly ground black pepper. Add 3 tablespoons of salad oil.

When dressing thickens, taste for correct seasoning ; if it is sharp yet oily, add more salt. Quantities should be in the ratio of 1 part vinegar to 2 parts oil. For **vinaigrette dressing,** add freshly chopped herbs of choice.

Gelatine

As gelatine setting strength varies according to brand, it is essentiel to follow instructions given on the pack. For instance, Davis gelatine recommend 1 oz to set 2 pints of liquid.

Mayonnaise

2 egg yolks
salt and pepper
dry mustard
$\frac{3}{4}$ cup salad oil
2 tablespoons wine vinegar

This recipe will make $\frac{1}{2}$ pint of mayonnaise.

Method
Work egg yolks and seasonings with a small whisk or wooden spoon in a bowl until thick ; then start adding the oil drop by drop. When 2 tablespoons of oil have been added this mixture will be very thick. Now carefully stir in 1 teaspoon of the vinegar.

The remaining oil can then be added a little more quickly, either 1 tablespoon at a time and beaten thoroughly between each addition until it is absorbed, or in a thin steady stream if you are using an electric beater.

When all the oil has been absorbed, add remaining vinegar to

taste, and extra salt and pepper as necessary.

To thin and lighten mayonnaise, add a little hot water. For a coating consistency, thin with a little cream or milk.

Eggs should not come straight from the refrigerator. If oil is cloudy or chilled, it can be slightly warmed.

Mock hollandaise sauce

2 oz butter
1 tablespoon plain flour
$\frac{1}{2}$ pint water (boiling)
1-2 egg yolks
salt and pepper
good squeeze of lemon juice

Method
Melt a good $\frac{1}{2}$ oz of butter in a pan, stir in the flour off the heat and when smooth pour on all the boiling water, stirring or whisking briskly all the time.

Now add egg yolks and remaining butter in small pieces, stirring it well in. Season and add lemon juice.
Watchpoint If the water is really boiling it will cook flour. On no account bring sauce to the boil as this will give it an unpleasant gluey taste.

Puff pastry

8 oz plain flour
pinch of salt
8 oz butter
1 teaspoon lemon juice
scant $\frac{1}{4}$ pint water (ice cold)

Method
Sift flour and salt into a bowl. Rub in a piece of butter the size of a walnut. Add lemon juice to water, make a well in centre of flour and pour in about two-thirds of the liquid. Mix with a palette, or round-bladed, knife. When the dough is beginning to form, add remaining water.

Turn out the dough on to a marble slab, a laminated-plastic work top, or a board, dusted with flour. Knead dough for 2-3 minutes, then roll out to a square about $\frac{1}{2}-\frac{3}{4}$ inch thick.

Beat butter, if necessary, to make it pliable and place in centre of dough. Fold this up over butter to enclose it completely (sides and ends over centre like a parcel). Wrap in a cloth or piece of grease-proof paper and put in the refrigerator for 10-15 minutes.

Flour slab or work top, put on dough, the join facing upwards, and bring rolling pin down on to dough 3-4 times to flatten it slightly.

Now roll out to a rectangle about $\frac{1}{2}-\frac{3}{4}$ inch thick. Fold into three, ends to middle, as accurately as possible, if necessary pulling the ends to keep them rectangular. Seal the edges with your hand or rolling pin and turn pastry half round to bring the edge towards you. Roll out again and fold in three (keep a note of the 'turns' given). Set pastry aside in refrigerator for 15 minutes.

Repeat this process twice, giving a total of 6 turns with a 15 minute rest after each two turns. Then leave in the refrigerator until wanted.

Baking blind

Chill pastry case, line with crumpled greaseproof paper and three-parts fill with uncooked rice or beans. An 8-inch diameter flan ring holding a 6-8 oz quantity of pastry should cook for about 26 minutes in an oven at 400°F or Mark 6. Take out paper and beans for last 5 minutes baking.

Savoury shortcrust pastry

4 oz plain flour
salt and pepper
pinch of cayenne pepper
2 oz shortening
$\frac{1}{2}$ oz Parmesan cheese (grated)
$\frac{1}{2}$ egg yolk (mixed with 1
  tablespoon water)

Use this pastry for canapés, small boat moulds and tartlet tins.

This quantity will make about twelve 1$\frac{1}{4}$-inch diameter canapés, or fill 12-16 boat moulds or tartlet tins.

Method
Sift the flour with seasonings, rub the shortening into the flour until the mixture resembles breadcrumbs. Add the cheese and mix to a dough with the egg yolk and water.

Chill the pastry dough for 30 minutes before using. Roll out to $\frac{1}{4}$ inch thick and stamp into rounds 1$\frac{1}{4}$ inches in diameter.

Place on a baking sheet lined with greaseproof paper, or line the dough into boat moulds or tartlet tins. Bake for 7-8 minutes in a moderate oven, pre-set at 375°F or Mark 5.

Watchpoint It is most important not to put this type of cheese pastry direct on to the baking sheet, for such small canapés can easily become scorched in a very short time — in fact in the time that it would take you to lift the first half dozen from your baking sheet. By lifting the greaseproof paper lining straight from the hot baking sheet to a cooling rack you can remove all the canapés from the heat at once.

Rice fried

8 oz long grain rice
1-2 tablespoons olive oil
1 small onion (chopped, or sliced)
salt and pepper
1 dessertspoon soy sauce
2 eggs (beaten)

Method
Cook the rice in boiling salted water for 12 minutes. Drain well. Heat the oil, add the onion and cook slowly until it is just soft. Add the rice to the pan and fry until it is beginning to brown, turning it well and seasoning. Then add the soy sauce to taste and the beaten eggs. Continue to cook the rice, stirring it all the time until it is dry.

Stocks

Chicken stock
This should ideally be made from the giblets (neck, gizzard, heart and feet, if available), but never the liver which imparts a bitter flavour. This is better kept for making pâté, or sautéd and used as a savoury. Dry fry the giblets with an onion, washed but not peeled, and cut in half. To dry fry, use a thick pan with a lid, with barely enough fat to cover the bottom. Allow the pan to get very hot before putting in the giblets and onion, cook on full heat until lightly coloured. Remove pan from heat before covering with 2 pints of cold water. Add a large pinch of salt, a few peppercorns

and a bouquet garni (bay leaf, thyme, parsley) and simmer gently for 1-2 hours. Alternatively, make the stock when you cook the chicken by putting the giblets in the roasting tin around the chicken with the onion and herbs, and use the measured quantity of water.

Vegetable stock

1 lb carrots (quartered)
1 lb onions (quartered)
$\frac{1}{2}$ head of celery (quartered)
$\frac{1}{2}$ oz butter
3-4 peppercorns
1 teaspoon tomato purée
2 quarts water
salt

Method
Quarter vegetables, brown lightly in the butter in a large pan. Add peppercorns, tomato purée, water and salt. Bring to boil, cover pan and simmer 2 hours or until the stock has a good flavour.

Tomatoes (skinning and seeding)

Scald and skin tomatoes by placing them in a bowl, pouring boiling water over them, counting 12 before pouring off the hot water and replacing it with cold. The skin then comes off easily. Cut a slice from the top (not stalk end) of each tomato, reserve slices ; hold tomato in hollow of your palm, flick out seeds with the handle of a teaspoon, using the bowl of the spoon to detach the core. So much the better if the spoon is worn and therefore slightly sharp.

Glossary

Bain-marie(au) To cook at temperature just below boiling point in a bain-marie (a saucepan standing in a larger pan of simmering water). Used in the preparation of sauces, creams and food liable to spoil if cooked over direct heat. May be carried out in oven or on top of stove. A double saucepan gives a similar result.

Blanch To remove strong tastes from meat and vegetables by bringing to the boil from cold water and draining before further cooking. Green vegetables should be put into boiling water and cooked for up to 1 minute.

Bouquet garni Traditionally a bunch of parsley, thyme, bayleaf, for flavouring stews and sauces. Other herbs can be added. Remove before serving dish.

Butter, clarified Butter which is heated gently until foaming, skimmed well and the clear yellow liquid strained off, leaving the sediment (milk solids) behind.

Butter, kneaded A liaison of butter and flour worked together to form a paste (in the proportion 1 oz butter to $\frac{1}{2}$ oz flour). Added to the sauce in small pieces at the end of the cooking time. Useful when the exact quantity of liquid is unknown.

Court bouillon Stock made from water, root vegetables, wine or vinegar, seasoning and herbs for poaching fish or veal and making sauces.

Croûte Small round of bread, lightly toasted or fried. Used as a garnish.

Croûton Small square or dice of fried bread or potato to accompany soups.

Fleuron Small pastry shape, used for decoration, eg. crescent shapes, diamonds etc.

Infuse To steep in liquid (not always boiling) in a warm place to draw flavour into the liquid.

Julienne strip Vegetable cut to small strip about $\frac{1}{8}$ inch by $1\frac{1}{2}$-2 inches long.

Liaison Mixture for thickening and binding sauce / gravy / soup, eg. roux, kneaded butter, egg yolks and cream.

Marinate To soak raw meat / fish in cooked or raw spiced liquid (marinade) of wine, oil, herbs and vegetables for hours / days before cooking. This softens, tenderises and flavours, and the marinade can be used in the final sauce. Use a glass / glazed / enamel / stainless steel vessel to withstand effects of acid.

Mousseline A smooth, light creamy mixture, either sweet or savoury.

Panade Basic thickening for fish / meat / vegetable creams. Often a thick béchamel.

Paupiette Thin slices of meat / fillets of fish spread with a farce, rolled up and braised / poached.

Poach To cook gently in trembling (not boiling) liquid.

Quenelles Dumplings made with forcemeat and bound with eggs, poached in special moulds or shaped between spoons and dropped into boiling water.

Reduce To boil a liquid fast to reduce quantity and concentrate flavour.

Roux Fat and flour liaison, the basis of all flour sauces. The fat is melted and the flour stirred in off the heat before the liquid is added.

Salpicon Savoury mixture of shredded chicken, ham, game or mushrooms bound with a sauce and used for filling bouchées, vol-au-vents and other dishes.

Sauté To brown food in butter, or oil and butter. Sometimes cooking is completed in a 'small' sauce — ie. one made on the food in the sauté pan.

Scald 1. To plunge into boiling water for easy peeling. 2. To heat a liquid, eg, milk, to just under boiling point.

Seasoned flour Flour to which salt and pepper have been added. To 1 tablespoon of flour add a pinch of pepper and as much salt as you can hold between your thumb and two fingers.

Slake To mix arrowroot / cornflour with water before adding to a liquid for thickening.

Index

159